MW00655342

More reviews of....

JOURNEY FROM
MANY TO ONE

For many Westerners, the ideas contained in the Upanishads, the philosophical books of India, are puzzling, abstruse, and complex. In this extraordinary book, Swami Bhaskarananda leads readers step-by-step, chapter by chapter, to an understanding of the core of Vedic philosophy: the unity of being. The Swami accomplishes this spiritual journey through the skillful use of apt analogies and well-directed reasoning that make the philosophical concepts of Hinduism easily accessible. Readers will find that this book will open their minds to new and rewarding possibilities of thought, while providing an uplifting appreciation of their own divine nature.

—Terri Storseth, Ph.D.
Assistant Professor of Rhetoric, American University

I find this book on Advaita Vedanta to be a one of a kind master-piece that makes the abstruse truths of Advaita Vedanta and logical implications accessible to the layperson in simple language.

—Tim Harris
Marketing Director

Swami Bhaskarananda has achieved what few scholars of religion would attempt: a comprehensive yet approachable presentation of Advaita Vedanta. This book has effectively and successfully created an uncomplicated understanding of the most paramount religious philosophy of India.

—Albert Leopold Smith, Ph.D.
lecturer and author, Ojai, CA

Books by Swami Bhaskarananda

The Essentials of Hinduism : A Comprehensive Overview of the World's Oldest Religion

Meditation, Mind and Patanjali's Yoga : A Practical Guide to Spiritual Growth for Everyone

Life in Indian Monasteries : Reminiscences about Monks of the Ramakrishna Order

Reminiscences of Swami Brahmananda : The Mind-born Son of Sri Ramakrishna

The Philosophical Verses of Yogavāsishtha : An English Translation of Yogavāsishtha-sāra with Commentary and Sanskrit Text

The Wonder that is Srī Rāmakrishna : An English Translation of Srī Srī Rāmakrishna-Mahimā by Akshaykumār Sen

Ordering Information:
Viveka Press
2716 Broadway Ave E
Seattle, Washington 98102-3909
206-323-1228
vivekapress@vedanta-seattle.org

JOURNEY FROM MANY TO ONE

Essentials of Advaita Vedanta

by

Swami Bhaskarananda

Viveka Press

Seattle

Viveka Press, Seattle 98102

©2009 by The Vedanta Society of Western Washington

For more information write to:
Viveka Press
2716 Broadway Avenue East
Seattle, WA 98102-3909 USA
Phone: (206) 323-1228
Email: vivekapress@vedanta-seattle.org
http://www.vedanta-seattle.org/

Published 2009
Printed in the United States of America

Publisher's Cataloging-in-Publication
(Provided by Quality Books, Inc.)

Bhaskarananda, Swami.
    Journey from many to one : essentials of Advaita
Vedanta / by Swami Bhaskarananda.
    p. cm.
    Includes bibliographical references and index.
    LCCN 2008923587
    ISBN-13: 978-1-884852-12-1
    ISBN-10: 1-884852-12-2

    1. Advaita.   I. Title.

B132.A3B43 2009   181'.482
        QBI08-600114

*Dedicated to those who are
searching for the ultimate truth.*

ABOUT THE COVER

The picture on the front cover was painted by Mrs. Mira Guerquin of Bellevue, Washington, U.S.A. The inspiration for this painting is the following imagery taken from the *Mundaka Upanishad*, one of the main scriptures related to *Advaita Vedānta*. Through this beautiful analogy the *Upanishad* tries to explain how the *Jīvātman* (the apparent self) becomes one with the *Paramātman* (the real self or *Brahman*):

The *Jīvātman* and the *Paramātman* are like two identical birds of beautiful plumage, always united and known by the same name and clinging closely to the same tree (same body). One of them (the *Jīvātman*) eats the tree's sweet fruits (objects of sense pleasure). At first the objects of sense pleasure seem to be sweet and enjoyable, but eventually they taste terribly bitter. The other bird (the *Paramātman*) looks on without eating (like a witness, totally disinterested in worldly pleasures).

Seated on the same tree, the *Jīvātman* bird moans (due to its worldly troubles), bewildered by its impotence (helplessness). But when it thinks of the *Paramātman* bird and meditates on how serene it is and how glorious, the *Jīvātman* bird gradually becomes free from grief, as it finally realizes that it has all along been no other than the *Paramātman* bird. (The suffering of the *Jīvātman* is the result of his feeling of impotence. This impotence is destroyed by his knowledge of unity with the *Paramātman*. The grief of the *Jīvātman* is the result of his identification with his body-mind-complex.)

Contents

List of Illustrations

Preface

Over the many years of my stay in the United States I have often been requested by my friends and members of our church to write a book on *Advaita Vedānta*. They said to me, "Swami, we find most books on *Advaita Vedānta* written by other authors difficult to understand. Why don't you write an easily understandable book on *Advaita Vedānta*?" I have written this book in response to their request.

Many of them, who are from a non-Hindu background, find it hard to accept truths validated mainly by Hindu scriptures such as the *Vedas*. Others, without any particular religious allegiance, cannot accept truths and religious ideas merely on faith. They can only accept what appeals to their sense of reason.

This book has been written mainly for such readers. I have tried my best to make the book reader-friendly, using mainly reasoning to present the ideas of *Advaita Vedānta*. At the same time I have taken care not to indulge in oversimplification. I have made sure that the readers will not be deprived of the opportunity of becoming acquainted with all the vital aspects of *Advaita Vedānta*.

In the publication of this book the following persons have helped immensely, and I acknowledge their loving assistance with deep gratitude.

Allen R. Freedman, Ph. D., for computer typesetting the manuscript.

Mira Guerquin for designing and illustrating the cover and drawing the picture of Shankarāchārya.

Charles Mathias for drawing the pictures of Rāmānujāchārya and Madhvāchārya.

Devra Freedman and Stafford Smith for proofreading and editing.

I shall feel greatly rewarded if this book proves to be helpful to those for whom it is intended.

Swami Bhaskarananda

Pronunciation Guide

Sanskrit words have been carefully and consistently transliterated (according to the chart below) hoping that the correct, or at least close, pronunciation will thus be indicated.

In this book all Sanskrit words, except for the names of persons, have been set in italics.

a is to be pronounced as *"o"* in *come*

ā is to be pronounced as in *star*

e is to be pronounced as in *bed*

i is to be pronounced as in *sit*

ī is to be pronounced as in *machine*

o is to be pronounced as in *note*

u is to be pronounced as in *pull*

ū is to be pronounced as in *intrude*

ai is to be pronounced as in *aisle*

au is to be pronounced as *"ow"* in now

bh is to be pronounced as in *abhor*

ch is to be pronounced as in *church*

chh is an aspirated version of *ch*

d is to be pronounced as *"th"* in *thus*

dh is to be pronounced as in *adhere*

g is to be pronounced as in *god*

gh is to be pronounced as in *leghorn*

kh is to be pronounced as in *inkhorn*

p is to be pronounced as in *paternal*

ph is to be pronounced as *"f"* in *fine*

th is to be pronounced as in *thaw*

sh is to be pronounced as in *shall*

"Advaita is the highest truth."

Srī Rāmakrishna (1836 – 1886)

Srī Shankarāchārya (7th century A.D.)
The Paragon of *Advaita Vedānta*

Introduction

Philosophers do not take anything for granted

Once Bernard Mannes Baruch (1870-1965), economic advisor to the US Presidents Woodrow Wilson and Franklin D. Roosevelt, said, "I'm not smart. I try to observe. Millions saw the apple fall, but Newton was the one to ask why." In other words, most people are only passive observers; they take things for granted. They don't think deeply or ask probing questions. But there are a few people who do. Newton was one of them. His questioning led to the discovery of what we know today as the laws of gravitation. It is this inquiring mind of Newton that made him a scientist. Had he belonged to ancient times he would be called a philosopher.

Unlike most other people, philosophers don't take things for granted. Their inquiring minds use the words—why, how, who, which, what, when and where—as indispensable tools to drill through the outer layer of observed facts and arrive at the deeper truth or truths hidden underneath.

The search for unity behind diversity

It is natural for the human mind to try to arrive at *one* general truth from *many* particular truths. For example, we see that animals and human beings die, fish die, birds die, plants die, insects die, and so on. These are so many particular truths. From these *many* particular truths we can arrive at this *one* general truth: all living beings die. This one general truth expresses all those particular truths.

Discovery of unity behind diversity by Hindu philosophers

In ancient times some Hindu philosophers in India wanted to arrive at a single truth that could explain this manifold creation. A very small number of those thinkers were somehow able to transform their minds into what we may call extraordinary or "pure" minds. With such minds they were able to know that one truth that explained everything else. They called that truth *Brahman*.

The average human mind, no matter how intelligent, cannot know *Brahman*. Only a pure mind can know it in a very special way. The knowledge of this truth is the conclusion or end of all knowledge. Therefore, it is also called *Vedānta*—the acme or end of all knowledge (*veda* = knowledge; *anta* = end).

This truth is one, and thus is called in Sanskrit *advaita*, which literally means "devoid of duality." The Hindu scriptures, such as the *Upanishad*s, refer to it as *ekam-eva-advitīyam* (one without a second).

There is a school of Hindu philosophy which accepts only this "one and only" truth called *Advaita*. This school of philosophy is therefore known as the school of *Advaita Vedānta*. The reader can learn more about this school in chapters 4 and 5.

After coming to know *Brahman*, those Hindu philosophers realized that their search for that one truth, which could explain the diversity in the physical and mental worlds, had ended, and there was nothing else to be known.

Search for unity behind diversity by modern scientists still continues

Modern science also has been trying to find one single truth by which this manifold *physical* universe can be explained. At one time it explained this physical universe in terms of molecules. But as the search continued, it has tried to explain the physical universe in terms of atoms, then quarks, and last of all, superstring, heterotic superstring, membrane, D-Brane and their vibrations. But science is not yet able to say that its search for that truth has come to an end. So the search continues.

JOURNEY FROM MANY TO ONE

1

Understanding the One and Only Truth: *Brahman*

Brahman is all-pervading

Brahman is a Sanskrit word. It is derived from the verbal root *brih*, which means "to pervade." Thus, the derivative meaning of *Brahman* is: "one who is all-pervading." It does not, however, mean that *Brahman* exists in space. According to the ancient, pure-minded Hindu philosophers, *Brahman* is beyond this world of time, space and causation. That's why *Brahman*'s existence, which transcends this world of time and space, is called transcendental existence. To explain this, we can refer to our dream experience.

We create our dream world with our minds. But to create a dream world, we have to first be ignorant of this world that we experience during the waking state. In other words, we must first transcend our *awareness* of the time and space that belong to this world. Thereafter, our existence as the dreamer will be in the time and space of our dream world. In this sense, our existence in the dream world could be called transcendental existence in relation to our existence in this world.

Similarly, according to the pure-minded Hindu philosophers, *Brahman*'s existence transcends not only the time and space of the world of our waking experience, but also the time and space of the world of our dream experience.

Brahman is infinity, eternity and changelessness

Brahman being all-pervading, as explained above, is beyond all limitations, such as those imposed by space, time and causation. Therefore, transcending space *Brahman* is infinity; transcending time *Brahman* is eternity; and transcending the ceaseless change generated by causation, *Brahman* is the state of changeless-ness.

Hindu philosophers say that as long as this world seems real to us, we live in a world of pairs of opposites. Everything that we know in this world belongs to a pair of opposites. For example, if we know joy we must know sorrow also. These two opposites constitute a pair. It is impossible to know one without knowing the other. They are always interrelated. To understand one it has to be related to the other. In this sense we can call this world a world of relativity and all the words and expressions that we use also belong to this world of relativity.

Darkness and light form a similar pair of opposites. Many years ago when I was in India, I got to know the principal of a well-known school for blind boys near Calcutta. He was born blind, but being very gifted was able to acquire high academic degrees from a prestigious university in England.

Once I asked him, "Do you *really* know what is called darkness?"

He replied, "No, I don't know it."

Then I asked him again, "Do you *really* know what we call light?"

He replied, "I don't know that either."

Then I said to him, "But as you are highly educated you must at least theoretically know what they are."

He said, "That's true. Reading and hearing about them have taught me that they are the opposite of each other. Having felt heat and cold and knowing them to be the opposite of each other, I can guess that darkness and light must be the opposite of each other in a similar way."

As said earlier, as long as we live in this world of pairs of opposites, we can only understand something by relating it to its opposite. So I can understand the word "infinite" only by relating it to the word "finite," and vice versa. It is not possible for my average mind to grasp anything that is not related to its opposite.

Transcendental *Brahman* is not related to anything else, because beyond the world of time, space and causation nothing exists other than *Brahman*. The use of the terms "eternity" and "infinity" is only a desperate attempt by the sages to give us a hint of the unrelated nature of *Brahman*. It is obvious that we cannot conceive of transcendental infinity or transcendental eternity with our impure, *finite* minds.

Had we been able to do it, coming within the confines of our finite minds, infinity would have ceased to be infinity.[1] That's why the Hindu philosophers will be satisfied if we can at least guess or *theoretically* accept these ideas.

Why *Brahman* cannot be correctly said to be infinite and eternal

We might ask, "Considering the limitations of our finite minds, why couldn't we honestly say that *Brahman* is infinite, eternal and changeless? Why should we say, '*Brahman* is infinity, eternity and changelessness?'"

In reply, Hindu philosophers will say, "Considering *Brahman's* transcendental nature, it will not be philosophically correct for you to say that *Brahman* is infinite, eternal and changeless. The words "infinite," "eternal" and "changeless" are adjectives. An adjective is used to qualify a person or an object.

"Personality is a limitation. Being free from all kinds of limitation, *Brahman* has neither a personality nor any other limitation. Therefore, no adjectives can be used to

---

1. The mathematical concept of infinity and the philosophical concept of infinity are not the same.

qualify *Brahman*. This is why you cannot say that *Brahman* is infinite, eternal and changeless."

For our sake, however, philosophers use words like "infinite," "eternal," etc.

Yet, for our easy comprehension, Hindu philosophers use adjectives like eternal, infinite, changeless, etc. in regard to *Brahman*.

Brahman is *nirguna*

The Sanskrit counterpart of the word "quality" is *guna*. What is devoid of any quality is called *nirguna* (*nir* = not, *guna* = quality).

Brahman, being beyond all limitations, is one without a second. A quality is contained in the object it qualifies. This kind of container and contained relationship can only exist when there are two. Since *Brahman* is the only one existing, there cannot be such a relationship. In other words, there cannot be any qualities in *Brahman*. That's why *Brahman* is called *Nirguna Brahman*. The word *nirguna* has another meaning. It is mentioned in Chapter 3 under the sub-heading: "Some characteristics of the pure mind."

Brahman alone is real

To understand why *Brahman* alone is *real*, it is absolutely necessary to understand what is meant by the word *real*. In Hindu philosophy, only eternity and changelessness are used to judge reality.

We might argue, "The Hindu philosophers must be wrong. Their definition of reality seems to be flawed. For example, I was a little baby once, and now I am grown up. Over the years I have undergone a lot of change, both physically and mentally.

"Aside from that, someday I'm surely going to die. Despite all these changes in me and the fact that someday I shall cease to exist, am I not real *now*?

"According to my thinking, whatever exists now must be considered real. As I exist now in flesh and blood, I can't but be real!"

In reply, Hindu philosophers will say, "We can prove that you also judge reality in your day to day life in terms of changelessness and perpetuity. Let us suppose you are looking at a strange creature that changes its form every five seconds. For the first five seconds it's a kitten. For the next five seconds it's a puppy. After that it becomes a weasel for another five seconds, and so on.

"Now, if we ask, 'What is this creature *really?*' you will surely answer, 'Since it has been changing every five seconds I don't know what it *really* is.' But had it not changed at all, had it remained a kitten all along, you would have no difficulty knowing that it was *really* a kitten. You would judge the *reality* of the kitten in terms of its changelessness.

"Now, let us suppose that you suddenly see a large, living elephant in your backyard, but you see it for only a minute. Then it melts away into thin air. So you conclude that you must have been seeing things. The elephant was not *real*; it was not really there. But had it stood there hour after hour, day after day, year after year, or forever, could you ever doubt its *real* existence? In this case you would surely have judged the reality of the elephant in terms of its *perpetuity*."

Transcending time, *Brahman* is eternity. Transcending space, *Brahman* is infinity. And transcending the ceaseless change generated by causation, *Brahman* is changelessness. Therefore, *Brahman* alone is real.

Brahman is formless and genderless

Forms can exist only in time and space. *Brahman* is beyond time and space and thus cannot have any form. Being formless, *Brahman* is genderless—neither male nor female. Thus, *Brahman* cannot be denoted by the pronoun "he" or "she." Therefore, the neuter Sanskrit pronoun *tat*, which means "that," is traditionally used to denote *Brahman*. Similarly, the neuter pronouns "it" and "which" also can be used in English to denote *Brahman*.

Brahman is indivisible

As *Brahman* is real it is changeless. Any division or part within *Brahman* implies change. Thus, *Brahman* cannot be divided. It is indivisible.

The word "division" is synonymous with the word "distinction." In Hindu philosophy, such as in *Vedānta*, three kinds of distinction (*bheda*) are recognized. They are as follows:

(1) *The distinction between objects of the same kind*, such as the distinction between one cow and another cow. This is called *sajātīya-bheda* in Sanskrit.

(2) *The distinction between objects of different kinds*, such as the distinction between a cow and a horse. This is called *vijātīya-bheda*.

(3) *The distinction between different parts of the same object*, such as the distinction between the tail and legs of the same cow. This is called *svagata-bheda*.

Brahman is beyond these three kinds of distinction. As *Brahman* is the one and only reality, there cannot be *sajātīya-bheda* and *vijātīya-bheda* in *Brahman*. In addition, *Brahman* is formless and does not have any parts. Thus, in *Brahman* there cannot be any *svagata-bheda* either.

Brahman is the Supreme Spirit

Matter and energy exist in the world of time and space. As *Brahman* is beyond time and space it cannot be either matter or energy. Many thousand years ago Hindu philosophers came to know that energy was only another form of matter. They also came to know that mind was also matter—only extremely fine matter. Therefore, *Brahman* must be different from mind as well. Judging by all this, we realize that *Brahman* must be the Supreme Spirit (*Paramātman*)—which is totally different from anything that is matter.

12

Brahman is True Existence

Brahman existing, everything else exists. *Brahman* is like the screen on which everything in creation has been projected like a movie. The existence of whatever we watch in the movie is due to the presence of the movie screen. Thus the existence of this manifold creation is none other than *Brahman's* existence. In the technical language of philosophy, *Brahman* is the substratum (*adhishthāna*) behind the creation. In other words, *Brahman* is True Existence (*Sat*).

Brahman is Consciousness

Brahman is Consciousness[2] itself (*Chit*). Every conscious entity in creation appears to have become conscious, as if by *borrowing* consciousness from *Brahman*, which is the one and only source of Consciousness.

Let us consider a person who is conscious. It may appear to us that both the body and mind of that person are conscious. We think that the body must be conscious, because it feels pain when pricked by a thorn. The mind must also be conscious, because it feels joy or sorrow.

---

2. It is necessary to understand the difference between the words "conscience" and "consciousness." Conscience is a function of the mind that enables you to know whether your actions are right or wrong. According to Hindu philosophy, it is a function of *buddhi* or intellect. On the other hand, consciousness is the state of being aware of something. It is the state of awareness of the mind.

But if we think a little more deeply we shall realize that the body cannot feel any pleasure or pain unless the conscious mind is somehow connected to it. The only function of the conscious mind is thinking. Thinking is knowing, because no one can know anything without thinking. Then again, willing or feeling is also no other than knowing, because no one can will or feel without knowing that one is willing or feeling. No other part of a human being other than the conscious mind is capable of knowing.

For example, suppose that someone has gone for surgery to a hospital. The surgeon first makes the patient unconscious by using chloroform or some other chemical. But what in the patient has become unconscious? Obviously, it is the patient's mind.

Losing consciousness, the mind is now incapable of knowing anything. When the surgery is performed, the unconscious mind is not aware of any pain in the body. When the mind regains consciousness, it becomes capable of knowing again. Only then can it feel pain. It proves that consciousness is not an integral part of the mind. Had it been so, it would never lose its consciousness.

We could argue that when the person was made unconscious, the old mind was destroyed along with its consciousness. It was no longer there. That's why the person did not know anything at that time. When consciousness is regained, a new conscious mind is acquired.

But this is not acceptable, because all the past memories are still intact in that patient's mind, except for the period when the patient's mind was made unconscious. This proves that it was the same mind.

The only valid explanation is that consciousness apparently *left* the patient's mind for a while and then *came back* to it. It is obvious that consciousness must have an unknown outside source from which it comes, and to which it goes.

The pure-minded Hindu philosophers knew that source to be *Brahman*. That's why *Brahman* is Consciousness itself. There will be more detailed discussion on consciousness in Chapter 8.

Brahman is Infinite Bliss

Brahman is also Infinite Bliss (*Ānandam*). Bliss or Ānandam is not joy derived through the senses. Experiencing sense-derived joy is called enjoyment.

Bliss is neither enjoyment nor suffering. It is beyond both. For example, let me suppose that I had a headache, and it hurt a lot. Half an hour after taking two aspirin tablets, my headache was gone, and I no longer was suffering. But even though my suffering had gone, was I then enjoying? No, I was neither enjoying nor suffering. I had gone beyond both. I had got relief from both suffering and enjoyment. This relief from both enjoyment and suffering can be compared to Bliss.

Suffering and enjoyment form a pair of opposites and belong to this world of time, space and causation. Therefore, Bliss, which is a state of relief from worldly suffering and enjoyment, must be transcendental. This transcendental Bliss is *Brahman*.

Brahman is the Absolute Truth

To understand that *Brahman* is the Absolute Truth it is necessary to have a clear understanding of what truth means.

In Hindu philosophy valid knowledge or truth is called *pramā*. According to *Advaita Vedānta*, valid knowledge or *pramā* can never be contradicted by any other kind of knowledge. In other words, it has non-contradictedness (*abādhita*). Any means of acquiring valid knowledge or *pramā* is called a *pramāna*. Hindu philosophy speaks of as many as six *pramānas* or sources of valid knowledge.[3]

Pramānas

1. Perception (*pratyaksha pramāna*). When we gain the knowledge of an object using only our senses as the means, then it is a case of sense perception or *pratyaksha*.

Human beings have five external senses: (i) sight, (ii) hearing, (iii) smell, (iv) taste and (v) touch. Besides these, they have an internal sense, which is the mind (*manas*).

Most Hindu philosophers admit two kinds of knowledge, immediate and mediate. When any existing ob-

---

3. Among the six major schools of Hindu philosophy the *Pūrva-mīmāmsā* and the *Uttara-mīmāmsā* schools accept six *pramānas*. The *Nyāya* school accepts four, while the *Sānkhya* and the *Yoga* schools accept three *pramānas*. The *Vaisheshika* school, however, accepts only two *pramānas*.

ject is related to any of the above senses, one acquires an immediate knowledge of the object. This immediate knowledge is called perception or *pratyaksha*. There are two kinds of *pratyaksha*: (i) indeterminate perception (*nirvikalpaka pratyaksha*) and (ii) determinate perception (*savikalpaka pratyaksha*).

When an object is related to any of our senses, at first there arises a bare awareness of the object. We simply know that *it is there* without knowing *what it really is*. This kind of perception is indeterminate perception or *nirvikalpaka pratyaksha*. For example, we may perceive a creature and become only vaguely aware of its existence. We come to know that it exists, but we do not know *what* it really is, what its qualities are, etc. In other words, we cannot determine what the creature really is. That's why it is a case of indeterminate perception or *nirvikalpaka pratyaksha*.

At the next stage of our perception we are able to determine *what* the object is with the help of our past experience. In other words, we now know this particular creature to be a cow, because we have seen a cow in the past. Had we not known a cow in the past, we would not be able to determine that the creature perceived was a cow. This is a case of determinate perception or *savikalpaka pratyaksha*. The determinate perception is expressed through such sentences as "This is a cow." or "That is a cow."

At the first stage we do not know the object of perception thoroughly or explicitly. At the second stage it is known explicitly. Nevertheless, what is known at the second stage *explicitly* is known *implicitly* even at the first stage. Only at the second stage, in the light of our past experience, are we able to *interpret* that *implicitly known* creature to be a cow.

In this interpretation we do not exercise our imagination. Had any imagination been involved in the interpretation it would not be called perception.

In simple language indeterminate perception is only sensing the object of perception, while determinate perception is the judgment of the object perceived.

2. Inference (*anumāna pramāna*). When we know an object not through direct sense perception but through external signs, then it is called a case of inference. Such perceived external signs and the unperceived objects must have an invariable relationship between them. Also this invariable relationship has to be "universal."

Let us suppose that we see a mountain at a distance covered by a dense forest. Then we notice smoke rising from a part of the mountain. Seeing smoke, we know that there must be fire on the mountain, because without fire there could not have been any smoke. There is an invariable relationship between smoke and fire. Wherever there is smoke, there must be fire.

We acquire this knowledge of fire using *inference* as our means, or *pramāna*. In this particular case, smoke is the external sign that helps us to *infer* the existence of fire.

3. Reliable testimony (*shabda pramāna* or *āgama pramāna*). Sometimes the testimony of reliable people is the means or *pramāna* for the acquisition of valid knowledge. The following example will explain this:

I was born at home in a city in India many decades ago. In those days it was not necessary to register the birth of a child in the city records. So I never had a birth certificate.

Before coming to the United States I needed to get a U. S. visa. To prove my age, the U. S. consulate in Calcutta asked me to produce my birth certificate, which I never had. Instead, I produced my certificate of graduation from my high school in which my age was recorded. The consulate wouldn't accept that document as the proof of my age.

Eventually, my mother had to sign an affidavit in the presence of a magistrate confirming my date of birth. This document was accepted as a proof of my age by the consulate. Only my mother's testimony was considered reliable.

Similarly, we acquire the knowledge of many scientific truths such as the existence of the subatomic particle called pion through reliable testimony. Being a subatomic particle it cannot be seen by the naked eye. Aside from that, it exists for less than 3 trillionths of a second. The knowledge of its existence can be acquired only through the testimony of scientists of proven reliability.

Thus, reliable testimony is one of the sources of valid knowledge.

4. Comparison (*upamāna pramāna*). Comparison is also a tool for our acquisition of valid knowledge. When comparison is used as a means, it is called *upamāna pramāna*. Let me suppose that I have seen water buffalos previously at my village home in India. Then I go on a visit to the United States. While traveling there I see a four-footed animal called a bison. Looking at the bison I first acquire the knowledge that this animal looks very similar to the water buffalos that I saw at home.

Then through comparison I acquire the further knowledge that the water buffalos at my home are like this bison. This knowledge *that the water buffalos at my home are similar to this bison* is not acquired through my present perception, because I do not perceive the water buffalos of my home *right now*. This valid knowledge I have acquired through comparison, not through perception, inference or reliable testimony.

5. Postulation (*arthāpatti pramāna*): Postulation is an assumption or supposition of an unperceived fact, which *alone* can explain something that cannot be explained otherwise. For example, there is an extremely truthful person named John who has taken the vow of not eating any food in the daytime. Yet he is seen to gain more and more weight. The *only* explanation for his weight gain must be that he eats a lot at night. We acquire this knowledge through postulation or *arthāpatti*.

Postulation differs from inference in that it is based entirely on logical conclusions, not on external signs.

Such knowledge acquired through postulation is surely not gained either through perception or inference. Nor is it gained through reliable testimony or comparison. The knowledge that John eats at night is not acquired through perception since we do not see him eating at night.

It is also not a case of inference, because there is no invariable relationship between becoming obese and eating at night. We cannot say that the obesity of everyone must be related to eating at night.

6. Non-perception (*anupalabdhi pramāna*). How do we acquire the knowledge that something does not exist? The means of acquiring knowledge, using perception, inference, reliable testimony, comparison and postulation, do not help us to acquire this knowledge. Therefore, some Hindu philosophers assert that non-perception or *anupalabdhi* is the means or source of our immediate cognition of the non-existence of an object.

Knowing *Brahman* as the Absolute Truth

Let us now find out which one among all the above six *pramānas* helps us to acquire the knowledge of *Brahman* as the Absolute Truth. According to most Hindu philosophers this knowledge can be acquired only through reliable testimony or *shabda pramāna*, such as the testimony of the *Vedas*.

The *Vedas* are a wonderful collection of super-sensuous knowledge, including the knowledge about *Brahman*, discovered by pure-minded Hindu sages. No testimony is considered more reliable than the experiential knowledge of these sages. The *Vedas* declare that *Brahman* is Truth (*Satyam*). The *Vedas* also tell us that *Brahman* is *Satyasya Satyam*, the Truth of all truths. In other words, *Brahman* is the Absolute Truth.

Yet the intellectual knowledge of *Brahman* as the Absolute Truth is different from the experiential knowledge of the pure-minded sages. What experiential knowledge is, and how that can be acquired with the help of a pure mind, will be discussed in chapter 3.

Brahman cannot be described through words and cannot be known by an average mind

Only the *pure* mind can know *Brahman*. An average, *impure* mind can never know *Brahman*. Due to *Brahman*'s extreme subtlety an average, impure mind, no matter how intelligent, cannot know it. Aside from that, *Brahman*, being the most abstract, cannot be described through words, just as we cannot describe our abstract feelings like joy and sorrow, even though we experience them.

2

Nirguna **and** *Saguna Brahman*

Nirguna Brahman

An attribute or quality is a factor of separation. For example, the power of burning is a quality (*guna*) of fire. It separates fire from water, which lacks that quality. As *Brahman* is indivisible, it cannot accommodate any factor of separation, or quality, within itself. Therefore, *Brahman* must be free from qualities.

As mentioned earlier, the Sanskrit word "*nirguna*" means "without quality." That's why the expression "*Nirguna Brahman*" is used to denote the transcendental *Brahman*.

Since *Nirguna Brahman* is beyond time, space and causation, it is a non-doer. It does not act. Action is only possible in space and time. *Nirguna Brahman* is transcendental and thus actionless (*akartā*).

It is also a non-enjoyer (*abhoktā*). *Nirguna Brahman*, being the only Reality *without a second*, cannot enjoy anything. For enjoyment, both the enjoyer and the object of enjoyment are needed. In the oneness of *Nirguna Brahman* there are no objects of enjoyment.

Saguna Brahman

When we try to think of the infinite *Nirguna Brahman* with our finite minds, we unknowingly project the limitations of our finite minds on *Nirguna Brahman*. As a result, *Nirguna Brahman* appears to be finite to us.

The human mind can never think other than in human terms. It unknowingly projects human characteristics or qualities on *Nirguna Brahman*. Thus impersonal *Nirguna Brahman* seems to acquire a personality resembling a human personality, however glorified.

Impersonal *Nirguna Brahman* appears to become personal *Brahman*, or *Saguna Brahman* (*saguna* = with quality). *Saguna Brahman* is also called in Sanskrit *Īshvara* (Personal God). In reality *Nirguna Brahman* does not undergo any change or modification whatsoever. *Saguna Brahman* is *Nirguna Brahman* experienced through the veil of time, space and causation.

It is like a person looking at the blue sky through two pairs of glasses, red and green. When red glasses are used, the sky looks reddish. When green glasses are worn, the sky looks greenish. In reality it is only the viewer's colored glasses that project those colors on the blue sky. The blue sky does not change its color at all.

Similarly, the finite minds of people, like so many colored glasses, project their limitations on *Nirguna Brah-*

man. The changeless and infinite *Nirguna Brahman* appears to acquire limitations like personality.

From *Nirguna Brahman*'s standpoint *Nirguna Brahman* remains changeless. The idea of *Saguna Brahman* is therefore not the ultimate truth. It is relatively a lower truth. Nevertheless, *Saguna Brahman* and *Nirguna Brahman* are not essentially different from each other. Just as the reddish sky and the greenish sky are really the same blue sky, so also *Saguna Brahman* is no other than *Nirguna Brahman*. They are essentially one and the same.

As mentioned above, the personality of *Saguna Brahman* is a projection of the finite human mind on *Nirguna Brahman*. Similarly, the human mind projects fatherhood or motherhood or other human attributes on *Nirguna Brahman*. Thus *Saguna Brahman* becomes a father or mother.

From the standpoint of human beings posited in the world of time, space and causation, *Saguna Brahman* is the creator of this world. He is omnipotent, omniscient and all-pervading. By His mere will He manifests Himself as this manifold universe. Although formless, by His divine magical power (*māyā*) He assumes various forms. By His *māyā* He has created the world with its pairs of opposites, such as good and evil. Even though the world is no other than Him, He is beyond the clutches of good and evil in the world. He is like a cobra, which is not affected by the poison in its mouth. Its poison affects only others.

Saguna Brahman is not only the creator, but the preserver and destroyer as well. Creation, preservation and destruction go hand in hand in this world. *Saguna Brahman* or *Īshvara*, therefore, has three basic aspects: (1) the creator aspect, (2) the preserver aspect and (3) the destroyer aspect. These three basic aspects of *Īshvara* are given the names *Brahmā*, *Vishnu* and *Maheshvara* respectively. When *Īshvara* creates, He is called *Brahmā*. When He preserves, He is called *Vishnu*; and when He destroys, He is called *Maheshvara*.

As mentioned earlier, even though genderless, *Saguna Brahman* or *Īshvara* can be looked upon as both father and mother. According to the devotees' mental attitudes they can establish other relationships with *Saguna Brahman* as well. They can look upon *Saguna Brahman* as friend, child, or even husband or sweetheart, for such relationships are also nothing but mental projections on *Saguna Brahman*.

In the Hindu tradition many great women saints like Meerābāi considered themselves to be spiritually married to *Īshvara* or *Saguna Brahman*. They looked upon Him as their Divine Husband or Divine Sweetheart. Some saints of India, both men and women, looked upon Him as their Divine Child.

Many saints of Hindu tradition such as Kamalākānta, Rāmprasād, Srī Rāmakrishna and others looked upon *Īshvara* as the Divine Mother. Such relationships were purely mental and completely devoid of any kind of association with the physical body. According to Srī Rāmakrishna, the famous 19th century saint of India, such attitudes toward *Īshvara* can generate feelings of great closeness between *Īshvara* and the devotees, and thus hasten the realization of *Saguna Brahman*.

Īshvara is also the originator and upholder of the eternal moral order in this world. This moral order or basic law, which is called *rita* in Sanskrit, maintains and controls the regularity and orderliness of everything in this universe, including the stars and planets and all the natural forces.

This basic law or *rita* is impartial and applies to everything that exists in creation. If a king and a beggar jump off a cliff together into a deep gorge, both will die. Gravity is part of *rita* and is impartial to both.

Aside from the creator, preserver and destroyer aspects, *Īshvara* has endless powers or aspects. One or more of these aspects can be personified as a deity in Hinduism. For instance, when a Hindu thinks of *Īshvara* as the giver of knowledge and learning, that aspect of *Īshvara* is personified as the deity Sarasvatī. In the same manner, the deity Lakshmī personifies *Īshvara* as the giver of wealth and prosperity.

It should be clearly understood that the deities are not so many different gods and goddesses. They are the personifications of the various aspects of one and the same *Īshvara*.

JOURNEY FROM MANY TO ONE

3

Pure Mind—what it is

Understanding what is meant by *pure mind*

It was mentioned earlier that some Hindu philosophers came to know the one and only Truth called *Brahman* with the help of their pure minds. What is meant by "pure mind?" Without entering into great detail, what pure mind is can be explained using the following analogy:

Ice, water and water vapor—all three are the same chemical substance, H_2O. Yet they differ greatly in their properties.

Now, let us examine how much freedom each of them enjoys. Consider a large room with several glass windows on each wall. Imagine that the room is sealed from the outside. Nothing, not even air, can escape from inside.

If you put a large chunk of ice in the room, it will stay wherever you have placed it. It won't be able to move anywhere else. Among the three forms of H_2O it has the least amount of freedom.

If that chunk of ice melts down into water it will have much more freedom. It will then be able to flow and spread out on the floor of the room.

But if this water is transformed into water vapor, it will enjoy the maximum amount of freedom. It will be able to fill up the entire room and reach the glass windows on the walls. Not only that, being the finest of the three, it will also become invisible. Had the water vapor had the ability to see, it would be able to see through the glass windows what was outside the sealed room as well as what was inside.

An average mind can be compared to ice or water. Such a mind has many limitations. It cannot know anything beyond the domain of sense perception and the world of time and space. It cannot know what is going to happen the next moment or what happened in the remote past. Metaphysical truths, such as the knowledge of *Brahman* or the hereafter, are beyond the scope of such a mind.

But when that same mind is transformed or made pure through spiritual discipline, it becomes something like water vapor. Just as water vapor can reach the glass windows on the walls of that large room, so also the pure mind can reach the outermost frontier of this world of time and space. But, because it belongs to this world of time and space, it cannot go out of it just as the water vapor could not escape from the sealed room. It can only have a *glimpse* of what lies beyond. It can have a glimpse of *Brahman* existing beyond the domain of the world of time and space.

In this world of time and space the pure mind also can experience the immanence of the same *Brahman* as its invisible essence. Such a mind becomes all-knowing. It can know all the events of the past, present and the future. Through intense spiritual practice genuine sages or saints acquire such pure minds. With the help of their pure minds the ancient sages of India came to know that one and only Eternal Truth called *Brahman* which exists beyond the world of time, space and causation. Physical and mental suffering, mortality, and all kinds of fear belong only to this world of time, space and causation. In transcendental *Brahman* none of them is present. Thus *Brahman* is perpetual bliss, immortality and fearlessness.

Having come to know *Brahman* as the essence of everything and every being, they realized that in essence they themselves too were *Brahman*. Thus they went beyond all kinds of suffering.

One might object, saying, "I cannot accept that an average mind is *incapable* of knowing anything beyond the domain of the senses. For example, I *know* the existence of my ancestors who lived hundreds of years ago. I know that they must have been there. I haven't acquired this knowledge through sense perception. I know this through reasoning, because had they not existed I wouldn't be here now!"

But this kind of knowledge acquired through reasoning is *always* based on sense perception. For example, we know the existence of our parents, whom we have seen through sense perception. Our parents also must have known the existence of their parents through sense perception. In this manner, going backward in time and using inferential reasoning, we can come to know the existence of our ancestors. Had we had no *perceptual* knowledge of our parents, no amount of reasoning would have enabled us to know the existence of our ancestors who lived hundreds of years ago.

Aside from that, in some schools of Hindu philosophy the mind is also a sense organ. It is called the internal sense organ (*antah-karanam*). Since reasoning is a function of the mind, knowing something through reasoning is also sense perception.

One may argue and say, "Pure mind is also mind. Therefore knowing *Brahman* through such a mind should also be considered sense perception." In reply, Srī Rāmakrishna, a knower of *Brahman*, says that the pure mind is so different from an average mind that it can hardly be called the mind; it is as good as the Spirit.[1]

Some characteristics of the pure mind

In addition to what has been mentioned in the preceding paragraphs, the pure mind has certain special characteristics, such as: calmness; compassion; serenity; cheerfulness; clarity of understanding; the capacity

---

1. Srī Rāmakrishna used to say in Bengali, "Shuddha mon o shuddha Āttā ek." (The pure mind and the pure *Ātman* are the same.)

to understand the deeper significance of observed facts; the absence of confusion, lethargy, and restlessness; the power to concentrate intensely; the absence of selfishness, cruelty, anger, jealousy, lustfulness, and craving for wealth, name and fame.

The above characteristics indicate a state of mind with preponderance of *sattva-guna* in it. *Sattva-guna* is a technical term used in the ancient *Sānkhya* system of Hindu philosophy. According to this philosophical system, this world of time, space and causation is composed of three extremely subtle substances, called *sattva-guna*, *rajo-guna* and *tamo-guna*. All together they are called *prakriti*.

These three *gunas* are so subtle and fine that compared to them, even the mind, energy, and subatomic particles like electrons, neutrinos and pions are relatively gross. We can never perceive these *gunas* with our sense organs. We can only know their presence indirectly, just as we know the presence of electricity indirectly through the functions of electrical devices, such as the TV, an electric stove, etc.

Each *guna* has its own distinctive and unique qualities or characteristics. For example, *sattva-guna* is of the nature of joy. It also has the ability to reveal unknown things. Again, if we see calmness, serenity, compassion, unselfishness and contentment in a mind, we know that *sattva-guna* is predominant in it. On the other hand, *rajo-guna* causes activity, movement, restlessness, the tendency to dominate over others, jealousy, avarice, lustfulness, anger, etc. *Tamo-guna* causes mental and physical inertia, such as lethargy, confused thinking, sleepiness and senseless anger.

These *gunas* coexist, and yet each one constantly tries to subdue the other two to make itself preponderant. Through spiritual practice *sattva-guna* can be made preponderant in one's body and mind. When that happens the mind is said to have become pure. It is this mind that can know the supersensuous truth called *Brahman*. How the *pure* mind knows *Brahman* is described in the next section.

Brahman is beyond the *gunas* and *prakriti*. *Prakriti* is matter, while *Brahman* is the Supreme Spirit, which transcends matter. This is another explanation as to why *Brahman* is called *Nirguna Brahman* (*nirguna* = devoid of the *gunas* of *prakriti*).

The secret of *how* the pure mind knows *Brahman*

Before understanding *how* the pure mind knows *Brahman*, one should first know the Hindu concept of the mind. According to ancient Hindu philosophers, mind is matter—extremely fine matter.[2]

To know anything, it is absolutely necessary for any mind, whether pure or impure, to be concentrated on it. According to *Advaita Vedānta*, to know *Brahman* a pure mind has to be focused with 100% concentration on

---

2. According to them, energy also is just another kind of matter.

Brahman. That school calls this state of concentration of the mind *nirvikalpa samādhi.*[3]

Figuratively speaking, even though *Brahman* is formless, the pure mind in the state of *nirvikalpa samādhi*

---

3. According to scholars, *nirvikalpa samādhi* is of two kinds: (1) *abhyāsarūpā* and (2) *sthitirūpā*.

    Abhyāsarūpā samādhi is a highly concentrated state of the pure mind, which, as it were, has become dissolved in *Brahman* like salt dissolved in water and has *apparently* become one with *Brahman. Brahman* being Spirit and mind being matter, mind cannot *really* become one with *Brahman.*

    We know that salt particles dissolved in water do not penetrate the water molecules and become identical or one with them. They remain hidden in the intermolecular spaces in the water. Similarly, the pure mind dissolved in *Brahman* still retains its identity as extremely fine matter.

    A portion of this mind can later come out of *samādhi* and again become aware of this world. This phenomenon is called *special awakening* or *vyuth-thāna* of the mind.

    Those whose minds have had *vyuth-thāna* from this kind of *samādhi* must try to go back to *samādhi* again. That's why it is called *abhyāsarūpā samādhi* (*samādhi* needing repeated practice). In the words of Srī Rāmakrishna, who experienced different kinds of *samādhi*, it is like ferrying back and forth between the noumenon/absolute (*nitya*) and the world of phenomena/relative (*līlā*).

    Sthitirūpā samādhi (stable *samādhi*) is a state of the total manifestation of *Brahman.* Once manifested, it is never lost. This happens when the ignorance of *Brahman* is annihilated. [See Chapter 10—"Piercing the Veil of Ignorance"] There is no *vyuth-thāna* from this kind of *samādhi.*

    Nirvikalpa samādhi is called *asamprajñāta samādhi* by the *Yoga* school of philosophy.

35

takes the form of *Brahman* (*tadākāra-kāritavat*), just as salt takes the form of water when dissolved in it.

Salt has its own specific crystalline form. When dissolved in water it becomes invisible. Its form disappears. It becomes colorless, like the water in which it is dissolved. Similarly, getting dissolved in *Brahman*—becoming one with *Brahman*—the mind comes to know *Brahman*. This kind of knowledge is not like any other mundane knowledge. It is "experiential" knowledge. It is also called "supersensuous" knowledge (*atīndriya anubhūti*).

Nonetheless, we may argue, "We have come to know from the Hindu philosophers that mind is matter. *Brahman*, immanent or transcendent, is *never* matter. To differentiate *Brahman* from matter, *Brahman* is called Spirit—something that transcends matter. How is it ever possible for matter to become identical with *Brahman*, which is Spirit?"

This question can be answered by pointing out that although salt dissolved in water becomes invisible, its molecules still occupy the intermolecular space inside water. The salt molecules have not combined with the water molecules. So also the pure mind, which is matter, has not really combined with *Brahman*—the Spirit.

Still another question remains to be answered: How can the sage's pure mind that is dissolved in *Brahman* be brought back to the awareness of this world and used to give teachings about *Brahman*?

This can be answered using another analogy from chemistry. Let me suppose I have put one teaspoonful of salt in a glass of water. If I stir the mixture, the salt will dissolve in the water. If I add more and more salt and keep on stirring, I shall soon notice that no more salt is getting dissolved. In other words, I have created a "super-saturated" solution of salt in water. Now let me separate the undissolved salt from this super-saturated solution through filtration.

If I now put a single crystal of salt into the glass containing this supersaturated solution, something very strange will start happening. Some of the salt in the supersaturated solution will come out as crystals and settle at the bottom of the glass. But not all the salt in the solution will reemerge as crystals. Only a small portion will come out. The rest will still remain dissolved in the water.

In this analogy salt is the pure mind of a sage and water is *Brahman*. While in *nirvikalpa samādhi,* the sage's mind melts away in *Brahman* as though forming a supersaturated solution. As the sage's mind is pure, it has a preponderance of *sattva-guna* in it. Therefore, it is naturally endowed with qualities like compassion, unselfish love, etc.

Sometimes the sage's mind retains only a single compassionate thought (*lesha avidyā*), such as a wish to alleviate the suffering of humanity. This thought of compassion acts as the crystal, which starts the process of recrystallization. When that happens, a small portion of the sage's mind that is dissolved in *Brahman* comes out like recrystallized salt. In other words, a portion of the sage's mind becomes aware of this world of time and space again. The rest still remains in communion with *Brahman*. The compassionate sage uses this recrystallized mind to teach others about *Brahman*, because he knows that by knowing *Brahman* one goes beyond pain and suffering forever.

Who is a *Jīvanmukta*?

The sage described above is a *jīvanmukta* (one who is liberated here and now). An analogy may help the reader to get a clearer idea about such a *jīvanmukta*. Consider a hypothetical submarine that is conscious like a living being. Even while submerged in the sea its periscope remains above the water. The submarine can observe what's under the surface with its powerful underwater light. At the same time it sees what's above the water with its periscope.

In this analogy the submarine represents the *jīvanmukta*; the underwater domain of the sea represents this world of time, space and causation; and the domain above the surface of the sea represents transcendental *Brahman*. The periscope represents the portion of the *jīvanmukta*'s mind that is dissolved in transcendental *Brahman*. The sighting of underwater objects by the submarine represents the interaction of the recrystallized portion of the *jīvanmukta*'s mind within this world of time, space and causation.

3 PURE MIND—WHAT IT IS

According to *Advaita Vedānta* a *jīvanmukta,* or one who is liberated here and now, has realized that *Brahman* alone is real and the world is illusory. Therefore, one may argue that after that experience of *Brahman* there should not be any awareness of the physical body or the world around it. But the continuance of the physical body or the world is not incompatible with the idea of liberation according to *Advaita Vedānta.*

Before liberation, one surely thinks of oneself as the body. After liberation, however, one realizes that the physical body and the world have only an illusory appearance. Even though they appear to exist they do not *really* exist. From the viewpoint of *Advaita Vedānta* liberation is only a change of perspective. Since the physical body is not real, its continued appearance, or its eventual disappearance, is no problem for the *jīvanmukta.*

To a *jīvanmukta* the body and the world are like a dream. The only difference between an ordinary dreamer and a *jīvanmukta* is that the ordinary dreamer, while dreaming, does not know that it is a dream. But a *jīvanmukta* always knows that he or she is the dreamer.

For the *jīvanmukta* the world experience is like watching a movie. Sometimes it is hilarious, sometimes sad, sometimes scary, but nevertheless always enjoyable because the *jīvanmukta* knows that nothing in the movie is real. The *jīvanmukta* may react to what is happening in the movie, just like any ordinary moviegoer does, but there is always that undercurrent of joy irrespective of what is

39

happening in the movie. That's why Shankarāchārya, the great philosopher saint of the school of *Advaita Vedānta*, says, "It is worthwhile to be born just in order to have the joy of *jīvanmukti*."[4]

In the dream movie that is this world the *jīvanmukta* may keep busy giving spiritual teachings to the dream persons. Even though the *jīvanmukta* acts, the dream movie must not appear to be real to the *jīvanmukta*, while an ordinary dreamer during the dream state keeps busy acting with and reacting to dream personalities thinking they are real.

---

4. In Sanskrit: *Jīvanmukti-sukhaprāpti hetave janmadhāritam.*

The Development of Different Systems of Hindu Philosophy

Hindu sages tried to describe the indescribable

We have learnt that pure-minded Hindu sages who had come to know *Brahman* wanted to teach others about it out of compassion. They also wanted to teach techniques that could help develop a pure mind. However, one may wonder how the sages could hope to give any teaching at all about *Brahman*, because *Brahman* is indescribable.

Sometimes little children spread their arms out wide to show how much they love their mothers. Yet we all know that love cannot be measured that way. Still, seeing that gesture we understand that they are trying to say that they love their mothers very much. Similarly, these compassionate souls talk about the indescribable *Brahman*, knowing fully well that transcendental *Brahman* cannot be described through the inadequate words and expressions of this world of limitations. They can only try to give us hints about *Brahman*.

According to Shankarāchārya, statements like "*Brahman* is True Existence, Consciousness and Infinite Bliss" (*Sat-Chit-Ānandam*) are not descriptions of *Brahman*. They are only so many hints or pointers about *Brahman*.

The sages gave their teachings orally

Initially the Hindu sages did not put down those eternal truths in any book. They taught those truths or *veda* (knowledge) orally to their students. That's why *veda* also came to be known as *shruti*—something that must be *heard* to be learnt (the word *shruti* literally means hearing). Students had to *hear* the truths from their teachers' mouths and memorize them.

Great emphasis was therefore put on developing a keen memory through the practice of celibacy. Celibacy (*brahmacharya* in Sanskrit) is the conservation of physical and mental energy by exercising restraint over certain mental and physical impulses.

Yet the ancient pure-minded sages who experienced the eternal truths did not develop any systems of philosophy. They only tried to express to others the eternal truths that they had come to know with their pure minds.

Sage Krishna-dvaipāyana compiled the *Veda* in a book

Eventually, hundreds of years later, a need was felt to record the vast mass of this accumulated eternal knowledge or *veda* in a book. A great sage named Krishna-dvaipāyana, who was endowed with a photographic memory, collected all this knowledge from people's "memory banks" as it were, and compiled them as chronologically as possible in a book. The book is also called *Veda*. With the help of his four disciples he divided the *Veda* into four parts: *Rik-Veda*, *Sāma-Veda*, *Yajur-Veda* and *Atharva-Veda*. This is why *Veda* is usually mentioned in English as the *Vedas*. For this monumental compilation work Sage Krishna-dvaipāyana came to be known as Veda-vyāsa or Vyāsa (compiler or divider of the *Veda*). He is also known as Bādarāyana.

The *Upanishads*

The *Vedas* contain some highly philosophical portions known as the *Upanishads*. The *Upanishads* are also called *Vedānta*—the acme or culmination of knowledge. Most of the 108 *Upanishads* talk about the oneness of the individual soul with *Brahman*.

The sages, due to the different degrees of purity of their minds, came to understand the same ultimate truth differently (*Ekam sadviprā bahudhā vadanti*)

In the Hindu tradition a person who has experienced *Brahman* is called a *brahmavid* (literally: a knower of *Brahman*). But one superior to a *brahmavid* is called a *brahmavid-vara*. Similarly, in the ascending order of superiority come the words *brahmavid-varīān* and *brahmavid-varishtha*. Among all these knowers of *Brahman*, the *brahmavid-varishtha* is the one whose mind has attained the highest level of knowledge.

These four different categories indicate that the sages experienced the same *Brahman* differently because of the different levels of purity of their minds. It is like a person who is traveling from the earth toward the sun in a space vehicle. At different distances the traveler takes pictures of the sun with a camera. Then the traveler returns to earth and develops the pictures. Although they are pictures of the same sun they look very different from one another.

Similarly, the minds of different sages with different degrees of purity experienced the same ultimate truth or *Brahman* differently. Thus, according to some sages the highest truth was *Saguna Brahman*, while others thought that *Saguna Brahman* was a relatively lower truth and *Nirguna Brahman* was the highest.

All these ideas found place in the mass of knowledge called the *Veda*. Some of the ideas were apparently contradictory to one other. For example, in the *Taittirīya Upanishad* we read the statement, "*Asadvā idamagra āsīt; tato vai sada-jāyata*," which literally means: "In the beginning there was no *existence*. From that (non-existence) *existence* was born."[1]

Then in the *Chhāndogya Upanishad* we read "*Sadeva somyedamagra āsīd-ekamevā-dvitīyam.*" Here we find a teacher saying to his student, "O gentle one, at the be-

1. *Taittirīya Upanishad* (2/7).

ginning there was only *existence*, which is *one without a second.*"[2]

The sages who came much later founded schools of Hindu philosophy

Such apparently contradictory statements must have created confusion in the minds of people. That's why some sages who appeared on the stage much later had to develop their own schools of philosophy to justify the rational basis of their individual understanding of the Vedic truths. This explains how different schools of philosophy developed in India.

In hinduism *philosophy* has a different meaning

The etymological meaning of the word philosophy is "love of knowledge." Philosophy tries to know the true nature of things that directly or indirectly concern human beings at the various levels of their existence. The purpose of Hindu philosophy is to enable truth-seekers to arrive at "the vision of truth" (*tattva-darshana*) [*tattva* = truth; *darshana* = seeing/directly experiencing]. This vision of truth is the *direct experience* of truth. For this reason, in Hindu philosophy the Sanskrit counterpart of the English word "philosophy" is *darshana*.

For example, consider a person named John. He has never suffered from a toothache, but has only heard and

2. *Chhāndogya Upanishad* (6/2/1).

JOURNEY FROM MANY TO ONE

read about it. By reading medical books he has come to *know* that sometimes cavities can develop in people's teeth due to certain germs living in the mouth. He also has come to *know* that when such cavities appear, the nerves inside the teeth become exposed and often get infected by those germs. When that happens, one suffers from toothache.

Thus John has acquired a fair *intellectual* knowledge about what a toothache is. But when he himself suffers from a toothache, he acquires the knowledge of toothache through *direct experience* [*anubhava* or *aparoksha anubhūti* (*anubhūti* = experience)]. It is this kind of knowledge that is called *darshana* (*darshana* = seeing/directly experiencing) in Hinduism.

Hinduism has six major systems of philosophy or *darshanas*

Six major and many minor systems of religious philosophy, some of which are among the oldest in the world, have developed within Hinduism. The major systems are as follows:

(i) The *Sānkhya* system of Kapila.

(ii) The *Mīmāmsā* or *Pūrva Mīmāmsā* system based mainly on the *sūtra*s (aphorisms) of Jaimini.

(iii) The *Vedānta* or *Uttara-Mīmāmsā* system based on the *Brahma-sūtra* (aphorisms on *Brahman*) of Bādarāyana or Vyāsa.[3] This system is based on the scriptures known as *Vedānta* or the *Upanishads*, whence the name. It is a special technical use of the word *Vedānta*.

(iv) The *Nyāya* system of Gautama.

(v) The *Vaisheshika* system of Kanāda.

(vi) The *Yoga* System of Patanjali.

Among the above, the *Sānkhya* system is the most ancient. Some of these systems have several branches.

Branches of the *Vedānta* system

The *Vedānta* system has the following branches:

(i) *Advaita* or *Kevalādvaita* school of Shankarāchārya [Shankara+āchārya (teacher)]. Also known as *Advaita Vedānta*.

(ii) *Dvaita* school of Madhvāchārya . (*Madhvāchārya* is also known as *Ānandatīrtha*).

(iii) *Bhedābheda* school of Bhāskarāchārya.

(iv) *Achintya-Bhedābheda* school of Baladeva. (Some scholars believe Srī Chaitanya founded this school.)

(v) *Dvaitādvaita* school of Nimbārkāchārya.

(vi) *Shuddhādvaita* school of Vallabhāchārya.

(vii) *Vishishtādvaita* school of Rāmānujāchārya.

---

3. Bādarāyana, Vyāsa and Krishna-dvaipāyana are one and the same person.

(viii) *Shaiva-Vishishtādvaita* school of Shrīkantha.

(ix) *Visheshādvaita* school of Shrīpati.

(x) *Sāmanjasya* school of Vijnānabhikshu.

(xi) *Shākta-Vishishtādvaita* school of Panchānana.

(xii) *Shāktādvaita* school of Hārītāyana.

According to some scholars, the *Vedānta* system has modern branches as well. For example, there is the Neo-*Vedānta* school based on the teachings of Swāmi Vivekānanda.

Among these various schools of the *Vedānta* system, the *Advaita*, *Dvaita* and *Vishishtādvaita* schools are most well known. In this book mainly the *Advaita* school, also known as *Advaita-vāda* or *Advaita Vedānta*, will be discussed in greater detail. The other schools of the *Vedānta* system will be discussed when the need arises.

Some scholars, such as Sadānanda Yogīndra in his famous book *Vedāntasāra*, used the word *Vedānta* to mean *Advaita Vedānta*. That is why many simply replace *Advaita Vedānta* by the word *Vedānta*.

As mentioned above, Vyāsa wrote the book called *Brahma-sūtra*. *Brahma-sūtra* is also known as *Shārīraka-sūtra*. Several schools of the *Vedānta* system are based on the commentaries written on this book by different philosopher saints, such as Shankarāchārya, Rāmānujāchārya, Madhvāchārya, etc.

Two well-known offshoots of Hinduism, Jainism and Buddhism, also have highly developed schools of philosophy.

Among all the schools of the *Vedānta* system, only *Advaita Vedānta* most emphatically declares that the individual soul is essentially identical with *Brahman*. According to this school, *Brahman* alone is real, and nothing else is. This message of *Advaita Vedānta* is the message of freedom, fearlessness and immortality. A study of Chapter 5 will help the reader to understand *Advaita Vedānta* better.

JOURNEY FROM MANY TO ONE

5

Understanding *Advaita Vedānta*

In the study of any scripture on *Advaita Vedānta* it is necessary to first discuss four very important points called *anubandhas*. *Anubandha* means "an indispensable requirement" or "the essential qualification."

The *anubandhas*

The four indispensable elements or *anubandhas* are as follows:

(1) **First *anubandha*.** Having *competent students* (*adhikārī*) is the first essential requirement of a scripture. Without such students the study of a scripture will serve no purpose.

(2) Second *anubandha*. Having a *subject matter* (*vishaya*) is the second indispensable requirement of a scripture. Without a subject matter a scripture is useless. And what is the subject matter of a scripture of *Advaita Vedānta*? It is the oneness of the individual soul (*jīva*) with *Brahman*.

(3) Third *anubandha*. The third indispensable requirement is the *relationship* (*sambandha*) of a scripture with

51

its subject matter. A "scripture," according to defini-tion, should have the capacity to make its subject mat-ter, which is previously unknown to the student, clearly known.[1]

The knowledge contained in the subject matter is to be revealed to the student, and the scripture is its reveal-er. This is the relationship of the scripture to its subject matter. For example, the scripture of *Advaita Vedānta* must have the capacity to convey its subject matter—the oneness of the individual soul with *Brahman*—to the stu-dent clearly. Otherwise, it cannot be called a scripture.

(4) **Fourth** *anubandha.* The fourth essential qualifica-tion of the scripture is that it should fulfill the *necessity* (*prayojanam*) of the student. Without any necessity for it, why should any student want to study a scripture? Then again, what is this necessity that is considered so essen-tial? This essential need is to *directly* experience one's identity with *Brahman.*

Experiencing this identity, one becomes fearless. Un-fortunately, to live is to be afraid. As long as we live, we have all kinds of fear. Fear is caused by the *apprehen-sion* that we may be deprived of *what we don't want to lose.* We don't want to lose our life, health, wealth, youth, power, fame, honor, love, security, spouse, children, par-ents, friends, etc. Whenever there is a possibility that we

---

1. The definition of a scripture in Sanskrit is *ajnāta-jnāpakam shāstram.* It literally means "what makes the unknown known is a scripture."

may lose any one of them, we become afraid. Thus fear is caused by our relationship with others.

The *Vedas* say that fear is possible only when there are *two* (many) entities. When there is only one entity, there can't be any fear. For example, an unarmed person will surely be afraid if he confronts a hungry tiger in a forest. If there is no tiger, and he is the only one in the forest, he has no reason to be afraid. Similarly, his identity with the one and only *Brahman* will lead him to a state of fearlessness.

If we compare *Brahman* to an infinite ocean, then we, as individual beings, are like so many waves in it. Each wave has its own finite form and name (such as "a large wave," "a small wave," etc.). Its individuality is based on its form and name—both of which are finite. Due to its sense of individuality it thinks that it is different from the other waves. Nor does it know that all waves are no other than the ocean. If the waves subside, they all lose their forms and names. They lose their limited, puny individualities and become one with the infinite ocean. Similarly, by losing our false, little individualities we shall gain our true individuality—which is *Brahman*-ness.

All kinds of suffering are caused by a sense of limitation. Whenever we feel limited in our health, wealth, fame, power and position, joy, etc., we suffer mentally.

But nobody *wants* to suffer. Thus there is an inherent tendency in all of us to go beyond our limitations. That's why a millionaire wants to be a multimillionaire, a scholar wants to get the prestigious Nobel Prize and a senator wants to be President.

Average people get joy when they earn a lot of money. Why does money make them happy? If we analyze, we shall see that money is no other than potential enjoyment, since it can easily be converted into objects of sense enjoyment.

Consider a hypothetical person who has earned 100 billion dollars. This money must have made that person exceedingly happy. But not for long. At some point that person will crave more and more money.

Why is the craving for money insatiable? It seems that the joy derived from a finite amount of money, no matter how great, will never give complete satisfaction. It seems that not until that person acquires an *infinite* amount of money and thus finds infinite joy will that person be satisfied.

We all know that in this world of limitations it is impossible to ever earn a limitless amount of money. Surely our hypothetical person also understands that. Yet the craving remains!

Advaita Vedānta says that this craving for infinite joy must be our true *nature*, just as it is the nature of a duckling to want to go to water and swim in it. It cannot do otherwise.

Advaita Vedānta reminds us that *Brahman* is beyond all kinds of *limitation*, and is *infinite bliss*. This *Brahman* is inherent in every one of us. An individual soul is no other than *Brahman*. It is our *Brahman* nature or inherent *Brahman*-ness that makes us crave infinite joy. For the same reason, a senator is not satisfied with the limited honor and power acquired as a senator and craves higher and higher positions of power, or a scholar wants to win the Nobel Prize to achieve greater fame.

Aside from all this, the vast majority of human beings suffer from a sense of inferiority. To compensate for this they want to be superior. Buying status symbols such as a large mansion on a waterfront in a posh neighborhood, a fancy yacht, super-expensive cars, Lear jets, Rolex watches, etc., only proves that the buyers are convinced of their inferiority. And they are somehow trying to feel superior through the acquisition of all these luxury items.

At the same time they are oblivious to the fact that through their actions they are only proving their sense of inferiority. Only those who are inferior want to be superior. Those who know that they are not inferior will never try to be superior.

The main doctrine of *Advaita Vedānta* is that we, as individual souls or *jīva*s, are *Brahman*. If we become convinced, even intellectually, that we are *Brahman*, we will lose our sense of inferiority.

If according to *Advaita Vedānta*, we, as individual souls or *jīva*s are *Brahman*, why then don't we *realize* our *Brahman*-ness? *Advaita Vedānta* says that the *temporary* ignorance (*avidyā/ajñāna*) of our *Brahman*-ness doesn't allow us to realize it. Because this ignorance is temporary, a proper teacher of *Advaita Vedānta* can help us get rid of it.

The fitness of a student willing to study a scripture

All are not fit to study the scriptures of *Advaita Vedānta*. One verse (6/22) in the *Shvetāshvatara Upanishad* says that a teacher of *Vedānta* must not teach it to anyone except his own son or disciple whom he knows closely. Another scripture instructs that none other than a son or a disciple should be taught the lofty teachings of *Vedānta*, because even the best medicine, when administered to the wrong person, may act like a poison.

Unfit students will not be able to understand the deep and profound truths of *Vedānta*. They may only understand them superficially. Or even worse, understanding nothing, they may imagine they have understood everything and start teaching others! For this reason, the ancient sages kept the knowledge of *Vedānta* well protected from the possibility of misuse by unworthy students. They would not give it to just anybody. That's how the truths of *Vedānta* came to be known as the *Rahasya Vidyā* (Secret Science).

The qualifications of students fit for the study of a scripture of *Vedānta* are as follows:

1. First and foremost they must have implicit faith (*shraddhā*) in their teachers and also enough self-confidence to believe that they will be able to understand the

import of the scripture with their teachers' help.

2. They must have studied the *Vedas* and the other books auxiliary to the *Vedas* and acquired at least a general comprehension of their subject matter. This will enable them to develop the yearning to study under a capable teacher and to understand the subject more deeply and thoroughly.

3. Either in this or previous incarnations they must have undergone various spiritual practices that have made their minds quite pure, serene and concentrated. Only such minds are capable of understanding the deeper meaning of the scriptural texts.

4. Having developed a burning spirit of renunciation, they have lost interest in sense pleasures derived from decorating their bodies, using cosmetics, indulging in sex activity, etc. They have no further desires for enjoying temporary immortality in heaven, because they realize that when their merits are exhausted they will have to incarnate on earth again as a mortal. Nor are they interested in any kind of celestial pleasure.

5. They have restrained the outgoing propensities of their minds (in Sanskrit such restraint is called *shama*), and brought under control their external sense organs (this restraint is called *dama*). At the same time, their minds and senses are focused on hearing (*shravanam*) the truths of *Vedānta* from their teachers' mouths in order to contemplate (*mananam*) and meditate (*nididhyāsanam*) on them.

6. They have acquired the ability to endure extreme heat and cold and other pain-bearing experiences in this world without even trying to prevent them (such endurance is called *titikshā*).

7. With their minds controlled through *shama*, they are able to concentrate them intensely. They are able to concentrate on the study of the scriptures as well as doing whatever is conducive to gaining the experiential knowledge of *Vedānta*.

In addition to study, giving various kinds of personal service to their *gurus* is also considered conducive to the acquisition of this knowledge. All this is called *samādhānam*.

8. And above all, they must have intense yearning to become free from all kinds of limitation (this yearning for freedom is called *mumukshutvam*).

Qualifications of a proper teacher

Any scripture of *Advaita Vedānta* will tell you that a proper teacher must be pure in body and mind and well-versed in the study of the *Vedas* and the knowledge of its import. Such a teacher is called a *shrotriya*.[2] The qualified teacher should also be *avrijinah* (free from sin) and *akāmahatah* (free from the desire for sense enjoyment). In addition, the teacher's mind should be centered in the one and only *Brahman* (*Brahmanishtha*). It also goes

---

2. This is the meaning of the word *shrotriya* according to Shankarāchārya.

without saying that such teachers must have great love and compassion for their students. They must also have the faith that capable students will be able to understand the import of the scripture with their help.

The method of teaching

Capable teachers give their teachings on *Advaita Vedānta* with the help of the following: (i) the reliable testimony of the *Vedas* (*shruti*), (ii) right kind of reasoning (*tadanukūla-yukti*), which is conducive to the acquisition of true knowledge and (iii) the personal experience (*anubhava*) of the student.

The word blasphemy doesn't exist in the Hindu tradition. Students can ask all sincere and honest questions about religion and spiritual life. Complete freedom has been given in the Hindu tradition to examine the validity of religious truths using proper reasoning conducive to knowing such truths deeply and exhaustively (*tadanukūla-yukti*).

But adverse reasoning (*tadviparīta-yukti*) with the intent simply to disprove these religious truths is not encouraged, because such reasoning does not help one to proceed along the proven path of spiritual inquiry. More importantly, great emphasis is put on *directly experiencing the truths* (*anubhava*)[3] rather than merely understanding them superficially.

---

3. See the example of "direct experience" given in the discussion in Chapter 4 under the subhead: In Hinduism *philosophy* has a different meaning.

The subject matter of a scripture of *Advaita Vedānta*

As stated earlier, the subject matter of *Advaita Vedānta* is the oneness of the individual soul (*Jīva* or *Ātman*) with the *non-dual ultimate reality* called *Brahman*.

Regarding this oneness questions may arise. One may ask, "Milk and water are two different substances. But when they are mixed together they become one. Are the individual soul and *Brahman* also two different entities like milk and water? Does their oneness mean something similar to a mixture of milk and water?"

In reply, *Advaita Vedānta* will say, "This oneness of the individual soul with *Brahman* is not at all like the mixture of milk and water. The *one and only* indivisible, all-pervading *Brahman* only *appears* to have become the individual soul, due to the ignorance of the individual soul, just as an ignorant person may think that the space enclosed within the walls of a room is different from the all-pervading space outside."

Truly speaking, *Brahman* alone is Real. It alone exists. Everything else only *appears* to exist. By the expression "oneness of *Brahman* with the individual soul (*Ātman/ Jīva/Jīvātman*)," *Brahman* alone is indicated. Therefore, the subject matter of *Advaita* philosophy is the eternal and indivisible *Brahman*.

One may further ask, "Yes, I have learnt that *Brahman* is real, eternal and changeless. I have also learnt that I, as an individual soul or *Ātman*, am identical with *Brahman*. But why do I not feel it? Why do I not *experience* my identity with *Brahman*?"

Advaita Vedānta is able to answer this question. But it expects the inquirer to first clearly understand what is meant by individuality or "I." In the course of the journey through *Advaita Vedānta* the reader in time will be able to know the answers to this and many other questions.

JOURNEY FROM MANY TO ONE

Understanding the Individual Soul
or the *Ātman*

If I exist, the world exists

As the story goes, once a young monk in India started screaming, "Help! The world is on fire!" Other monks rushed to him and discovered that only a part of his robe had caught fire.

After putting out the fire, they asked him, "It's only your robe that caught fire. Why were you screaming, 'The world is burning'?"

The monk replied, "If I am gone, where will the world be?"

It appears that if I do not exist as the knower of this world, the world does not exist for me. Conversely, if I, the knower of this world, exist, the world also exists. Yet, I can never be sure that the world that I know is not just a figment of my imagination. For example, as long as my dream lasts, the dream world appears to be so real. But when I wake up, I realize that the dream world was not real. It was never really there. It was nothing but a figment of my imagination.

How do I know that the world experienced by me in the waking state is not also a dream world, since it disappears when I fall asleep and start dreaming again? It could also be a figment of my imagination or a hallucination.

Thus, I can dismiss both of them, doubting the reality of their existence, but I cannot disprove my own existence as the doubter. Doubting is thinking. And thinking is knowing. As I am a doubter I must also be a knower. But for any act of knowing, three factors are essential—(1) the knower, (2) knowledge and (3) the object known. They form a triad. In Sanskrit this triad is called a *triputī*. Each of the three members of this triad is inseparable from the other two. All the three must co-exist. In the absence of any one of them the other two become meaningless.

Now, who is the knower? It is obvious that one who knows is the knower or the subject, and what one knows is the object of one's knowledge. But what is knowledge itself? We know that every action must have an effect. Knowing is an action. Therefore, knowledge must be the effect or outcome of that action.

So, it appears that the world of many exists only when its knower experiences it, otherwise not. Without a knower no object can be known. In *Advaita Vedānta* there is a theory called *Drishti-Srishti-Vāda* connected with this line of thinking. This theory is also called

64

Eka-Jīva-Vāda.[1]

According to this theory, seeing or knowing is creating. The world is created the very moment I see or know it. Both happen simultaneously. It is like the creation of my dream world when I start dreaming. I create the dream world the very moment I see or know it. Seeing and knowing the dream world happen simultaneously.

Since I am the knower of this world, I must be its creator as well. The world exists because I exist. In other words, there is only one individual soul existing, and that's no other than myself. There is no creator of this world other than myself. This individual soul or the *Ātman* is the real "I" or the "true self."

Who or what is this "I"? It is obvious that I must *know* it. Otherwise, I would be denying my own existence. As knowing is creating, have I created this "I"? In that case, to know or to create this "I," some other "I" must have already existed before it, and so on and so forth, ad infinitum.

Is there a first "I" in this infinite chain of cause and effect? If so, that "I" must be an *uncaused* or beginning-less

---

1. There is another theory called *Srishti-Drishti-Vāda*. According to this second theory, one can see or experience the world because it is *already* there. Its existence is not dependent on anyone's seeing or knowing it. Whether one experiences this world or not, it exists. This theory, *Srishti-Drishti-Vāda* (*srishti* = creation. *drishti* = seeing. *vāda* = theory), states that creation came first and then came seeing or knowing. The *Advaita Vedānta* school does not accept this theory.

"I," and this uncaused "I" must be eternal, because anything that has no beginning must also be endless.

Conversely, something that has a beginning in time cannot be eternal, because timelessness alone is eternity. What has no beginning in time is timeless. Being timeless, it is eternity itself. Therefore, what is beginningless must be endless or eternal. To say, "What is beginningless must have no existence at all," is true for only what exists in time and space. Alexander Friedman's model of the Big Bang Theory based on Einstein's General Theory of Relativity says the same thing. Along with the great explosion, or Big Bang, which caused this world, time and space were also created simultaneously. But what exploded? Whatever exploded must have existed beyond time and space.

Something that is beginningless should not be confused with something with an *unknown* or *unknowable* beginning. Anything that has a *beginning*, whether it is unknown or unknowable, must have an end also.

Advaita Vedānta calls this eternal "I" the *Ātman* or the *true* Self. As stated earlier, the *Ātman* is also called *jīva*. Aside from this, *Advaita Vedānta* says that when this world came into existence, time, space and causation also came along with it. For example, when I fall asleep, I create a dream world and a dream body. Simultaneously I also create "dream space" and "dream time." I then exist in the space and time of the dream world. I no longer am aware of existing in the time and space of this world that

I experience in the waking state.

Thus, anything that is created must exist within the domain of time, space and causation. The *Ātman*, being beginningless and eternal, was never created. Therefore, the *Ātman* or the "I" does not belong to the domain of time, space and causation. In this sense it has transcendental existence in relation to both the time and space of this world and that of the dream world.

We can know the existence of this "I" or the *Ātman* through other methods of inquiry as well. These methods of inquiry will be discussed in the succeeding chapters.

JOURNEY FROM MANY TO ONE

7

Method of Separating the Knower from the Objects Known

Posited as I am in this manifold universe, I have an inherent yearning to exhaustively know all that exists in the universe.

All that exists in this universe can be placed under two categories: (i) the knower and (ii) the objects known.

It is I who know this manifold universe. So, as its knower, I belong to the first category. The rest of the universe, being the object of my knowledge, belongs to the second category.

Thus whatever exists outside my body, such as the heavenly bodies, this earth with its human beings, animals, birds, fish, trees, plants, mountains, lakes, rivers, oceans, islands and continents—are all so many objects of my knowledge.

From common sense we understand that the knower and the object known cannot be the same. For example, I know my car. Therefore, I cannot be my car. In the same manner, I cannot be the stars, planets, and all other objects around me, because they are the objects of my knowledge.

I have my body, energy, senses, mind, intellect and ego. In *Advaita Vedānta* this package of body, mind, etc., is called the "body-mind-complex" (*dehendriya-sanghāta*). Let me find out what is my relationship with this package.

I am not my body

Am I my body? As I know it, it is the object of my knowledge. Therefore, I am different from it.

I am not my energy

According to physics, energy is the capacity for doing work. My vital energy enables my body and mind to work. Am I this energy? It can't be so, because although it is invisible I know its presence and its functions. Being the object of my knowledge it is different from me.

I am not my senses

Am I my senses? I know their presence and their functions. Being the objects of my knowledge they must be different from me.

I am not my mind

What about my mind? I know its presence and also know the various thoughts that arise in it. Therefore, my mind is also the object of my knowledge. As its knower I am different from it.

I am not my intellect

I know that my intellect is comparatively superior or inferior to the intellects of other people. Therefore, being the object of my knowledge the intellect is different from me.

I am not my ego

Now let me examine if I am my ego. Firstly, my ego is no other than my thought. It is an idea only. [It acts as a factor of separation in my mind. It helps me to separate myself from whatever I *think* I am not.] As ego is a thought, it is only a modification of my mind. As I am not my mind, I can't be my ego.

I know that my ego, which dwells inside my mind, is also an object of my knowledge. I know its nature as well as its functions. Sometimes it is stubborn, sometimes cruel, sometimes kind, and so on. It also thinks, "I did this" or "I enjoyed that." Thus, not only the ego but also its functions are the objects of my knowledge. I, therefore, cannot be my ego. I must be different from it.

I am not a doer or enjoyer

Thus it has been proved that being different from all of the elements of the body-mind-complex as the *knower*, I must exist independently. Even if they are annihilated, I exist. But as discussed earlier, the knower, knowledge and the object known cannot exist independently of one another. They must coexist. That being the case, if the objects of my knowledge, such as my body, energy, mind, etc., are annihilated, I can no longer exist as the *knower*. So no action including *knowing* is possible at that time. In other words, "I" must then be *actionless*. I am no longer a "doer."

I also know that without the knowledge of enjoyment there cannot be any enjoyment. Therefore, it follows that when I cease to be a knower, I have ceased to be an enjoyer as well. Therefore, if my body-mind-complex (*dehendriya-sanghāta*) is annihilated, I alone exist as the non-doer (*akartā*) and the non-enjoyer (*abhoktā*). This "I" is called the *Ātman* in *Advaita Vedānta*.

Finding the Source of
Consciousness

Even though I have understood intellectually through reasoning that I am not my body, energy, senses, mind, intellect and ego, still I often identify with them. For example, when my stomach is upset, I sometimes say, "*I* am not well." At some other time I may say, "My *stomach* is upset." When my energy level is low I say, "*I* am tired today." At another time I may say, "My *energy level* is low today." When my mind is upset, I say, "*I* am upset"; but at some other time I may say, "My *mind* is upset." But in the case of my ego, I seem to completely identify with it *all the time* as long as my mind is conscious. Let us try to know why and how this kind of identification happens.

Consciousness is not a quality of the mind

So far as my conscious mind is concerned, let me first find out if consciousness is its inherent quality. I know that the quality of anything is inseparable from it. For example, the capacity to burn is a quality of fire. It is inseparable from fire. Without this quality fire ceases to be fire.

Is consciousness inseparable from the conscious mind? It does not seem to be so; yet, if my mind is subjected to some chemical, such as chloroform, it apparently loses consciousness.[1] In other words, consciousness apparently *leaves* the mind. During this state of unconsciousness the mind cannot think or know anything.

The ego, being only a thought, is not there anymore. During its unconscious state the mind loses its awareness of this manifold universe as well. But as soon as consciousness apparently *comes back* to the mind, the mind starts thinking and knowing. Since consciousness does *leave* the mind sometimes and then *comes back* to it, it cannot be an intrinsic quality of the mind.

But one might object, saying that consciousness is an inherent quality of the mind and does not leave the mind at all. When chloroform is applied to it, the conscious mind becomes annihilated along with its quality of consciousness. Then again, when the effect of chloroform wears off, another *new* mind posessing consciousness comes and takes the place of the annihilated mind.

This objection cannot be sustained because the mind that regains consciousness has all the past memories and

---

1. According to Hindu philosophy, the mind is not the product of the brain. Hindu philosophy says that the mind can exist even without the brain. It only uses the brain as an instrument to make contact with this external physical world.

other character traits intact in it. Had it been a new and different mind, this would not have been possible.

Consciousness is different from the mind

Thus we know that consciousness is different from the mind. Besides that, when it apparently returns to the mind, consciousness does not combine with the mind as hydrogen and oxygen combine together to form a compound like water. Such combination is not possible because, according to Hindu philosophy, mind is a kind of fine matter while consciousness is the immaterial Spirit.

The presence of consciousness in the mind can be compared to the blue sky, which is being reflected on a mirror made of untinted glass. Although it may appear that the blue sky has combined with the mirror, it has never become one with the mirror. It is completely different from the mirror even when it appears to have become one with it. In this analogy the mirror represents the mind and the blue sky represents consciousness.

Then again, since consciousness *leaves* the mind and *returns* to it, it must move back and forth from *outside* the mind. I know that the mind and the rest of the manifold universe exist in the domain of time, space and causation. Does consciousness exist beyond the domain of time, space and causation, or does it exist within the world of space and time?

Consciousness is all-pervading, but not manifest equally everywhere in this world of time and space

Had consciousness existed outside the domain of time, space and causation, it would not be possible for consciousness to ever enter the mind, which belongs to this world of time, space and causation. One explanation could be that consciousness is all pervading, and this world of time, space and causation exists in it. Although consciousness is everywhere, it is not equally *manifest* everywhere. That this is possible can be explained with the help of the following analogy:

Let us suppose that in a room there are four 100-watt light bulbs. If I turn them all on, each one will give out the same amount of light. Now, let me cover the first bulb with one layer of paper, the second one with two layers of paper, and the third one with three layers of paper. The fourth bulb, however, I leave uncovered. Now, if I turn all of them on, will the same amount of light be given out by each one of them?

The answer, of course, is "No." But it cannot be denied that all of them being 100-watt bulbs, the same capacity for illumination must be there in each one. Only the *manifestation* of that capacity varies from one bulb to the other.

As mind is extremely fine matter, consciousness is usually more manifest in it than in grosser objects such as living plants or rocks. Yet, there can be situations when the manifestation of consciousness in the mind can be obstructed by the use of chloroform or similar chemicals. And when the effect of such chemicals wears off, consciousness becomes manifest again in the mind.

Even if consciousness is not manifest in the mind, is it still not possible for it to be present in the mind as its inseparable quality? No, it is not possible because, as mentioned earlier, consciousness is immaterial Spirit while mind is matter. Consciousness, whether or not it is manifest in the mind, is always separate from the mind. Therefore, consciousness can never be an inherent quality of the mind.

The mind is only an instrument to acquire knowledge; it is not the knower

As discussed earlier in Chapter 7, I am the *only* knower. My mind, being the object of my knowledge, is different from me and cannot be the knower. Yet it *appears* that the mind thinks and knows things. How can there be two knowers? I know that an unconscious mind cannot think. Only when consciousness comes into it or becomes manifested in it, does it think and know.

Strangely enough, when the conscious mind knows the manifold universe, I also come to know it simultaneously. Conversely, in its unconscious state, when the mind is unaware of this manifold universe, I am also unaware of this universe.

Am I then identical with my mind? The possibility of my being identical with the mind is ruled out by the logic that, as its knower, I must be different from it. Therefore the only solution is that *I am consciousness itself.* Without me the mind cannot know anything. I am using the mind *as an instrument* to know this manifold universe. Even though in my true state I transcend the world of time, space and causation, I have the ability to manifest myself in the mind, which belongs to this world of time and space. When that happens, I get to know this world, using the mind as my instrument.

The conscious mind cannot know consciousness

The above conclusion can also be arrived at from another angle of consideration. We know that it is the conscious mind that appears to know things. But does the conscious mind know consciousness itself?

It is not possible, because the knower and the object known cannot be the same. Accordingly, to know consciousness the conscious mind has to be separate from consciousness. But the problem is that when consciousness is not manifest in the mind, the mind devoid of consciousness cannot think or know anything. Therefore, the conclusion is that it is impossible for the conscious mind to know consciousness.

Again, the very moment consciousness becomes manifest in the mind, the first thought that arises in the conscious mind is the ego. Since the mind is at that time conscious, the ego, being a thought, must also be conscious. Apart from this, it appears that the conscious mind cannot know anything, such as this manifold universe, until the ego appears in it. And as soon as the ego appears, the mind becomes aware of this manifold universe. This ego in the conscious mind seems to operate as a factor of separation. That's why as soon as the ego appears, along with it appears this world of many.

Who experiences the world of many?

But who *really* becomes aware of all this? Who knows this manifold universe? It may seem that the conscious mind or the conscious ego alone knows it, because the awareness of this world of many becomes possible only when the ego is born in the conscious mind.

Further, the ego of the conscious mind seems to know this world *only when* consciousness is present in the ego, otherwise not. What role is played by consciousness in this apparent act by the ego of knowing this world?

One possible answer to this question is that it is consciousness that really knows this world of many. It only uses the ego as its instrument to know the world.

In physics when an ordinary iron rod is put in the proximity of a powerful magnet, it acquires magnetic power. The magnetic power thus acquired is called induced magnetism. As soon as the powerful magnet is taken away from the iron rod, the rod loses its magnetic power.

Similarly, the ego seems to acquire its knowing ability through induction from the presence of consciousness. The real power of knowing is centered in consciousness alone. And consciousness alone is the true knower.

I am consciousness itself

As discussed at the beginning of this chapter, I am the *only* knower of this world of time, space and causation. From the above discussions it can be concluded that "I" must be that consciousness which *induces* knowing power in the ego whenever "I" am present in it. When that happens I *seem to be* temporarily identified with the ego. At that time the ego, with which I have identified, *appears* to be myself. This ego is my *apparent* self only.

It is this apparent self that seems to know this manifold universe. In *Advaita Vedānta* it is called the *Jīva* or the *Jīvātman*, or simply *Ātman*. In relation to this *apparent self* the real "I" or the *real self* is called the supreme self or the *Paramātman*. This *Paramātman* is *Brahman*. So consciousness is *Brahman*.

Moreover, as the *real* knower, I am the *subject* and the *real* "I." The ego is the *object* of my knowledge and can never be the knower or the real "I." It is the *false* "I." The real "I"—the *subject* "I"—is different from it. Srī Rāmakrishna[2] calls this false *object* "I," the *unripe* "I." He calls the real *subject* "I," the *ripe* "I."

2. Srī Rāmakrishna (1836 – 1886) is one of the most renowned Hindu saints of the 19th century.

At this point the following question may naturally arise: "It was stated earlier that the "I" or the *Ātman* is "not the doer of any action" (*akartā*). But isn't *knowing* a kind of action? Yet, at the beginning of this chapter it was stated that the "I" is *the only* knower. How can these two contradictory statements be reconciled?"

To reconcile these two apparently contradictory statements we have to take the help of some analogies.

The *Ātman* experiences the world as a witness

The way in which the *Ātman* or the true Self or the *ripe* "I" knows anything is a very special kind of knowing. It can be called "witnessing" (knowing without getting actively involved). For example, the *Ātman* or the *ripe* "I" is like a newspaper reporter who is watching a game of soccer or hockey being played. He is not a member or supporter of either team and does not care which team wins or loses. In other words, he is not emotionally or *actively* involved in the game. He only *witnesses* what is happening in front of him. In this sense he is neither the doer nor the enjoyer.

Another analogy that can explain how the non-doer *Ātman* knows the world without getting actively involved is that of a fast-turning solid metallic wheel. As the wheel rotates, every part of the wheel moves except the center point. Remaining stationary at the center, the unmoving point witnesses, as it were, the movement of the wheel around it. This non-moving point can be compared to consciousness in relation to the activities of the mind or the ego. Like the point at the center of the moving wheel, the subject "I" or the ripe "I" *witnesses* the activities of the mind without getting *actively* involved with them.

Can consciousness know consciousness?

In any act of knowing there should be the triad consisting of the knower, knowledge and the object known. As there is only one consciousness, the question of consciousness knowing consciousness does not arise.

9

The *Ātman* is the Dearest and the Only Source of Joy

Now let us understand the *Ātman* from another perspective. Why are certain persons or objects dear to me? If I think a little deeply, I shall discover that no persons or objects are dear for their own sake. In other words, *dearness* is not an integral quality of any of them.

Whether they are dear or not is totally dependent on how I interpret them. For example, let me suppose that I am full after eating my favorite dish. Now, if someone forces me to eat more of that dish, it will be a torture for me. That dish will become most distasteful, if not totally disgusting. Yet the same dish was so dear to me when I was hungry. Now that my hunger is gone, it is no longer dear to me. Had dearness been an integral quality of that dish it would be dear to me at all times, whether I were hungry or not.

Then again a person who is very dear to me is not likely to be dear to my enemy. On the other hand, if that very person becomes a close friend of my enemy, he will no longer be as dear to me. The wife is dear to her husband, not for her own sake but for the husband's own sake. In other words, one who is dearest to me is no other than myself. I am my dearest. That's why anything or anyone that satisfies *my* need is dear to me. Even among all the closest members of my family, I myself am my dearest.

What is at the very core of my being is the *Ātman*. That's the real me. That *Ātman* is the dearest. Anything that is closer to the *Ātman* is dearer to me. My vital force (*prāna*) is closer to me than my body. That is why my vital force or life force is dearer to me than my body. For that reason, to save my life I may even agree to the amputation of my limbs.

Then again, mind is even closer to the *Ātman* than the life force. That is why one's mind is dearer than one's life. People sometimes sacrifice their lives out of patriotism or the urge to save their honor. Both patriotic feeling and the craving for honor are purely mental in character. These people gladly sacrifice their lives for their *mental* satisfaction because mind is closer to the *Ātman* than life.

In short, whatever is closer to the Self or the *Ātman* is dear. A man loves his own wife and children more than others, because they are closer to his Self than others. Whatever reflects the Self is dear. Whether someone or something is dear to a person is judged by only one criterion: Is the person or object close to his or her Self or the *Ātman*?

This idea has also been expressed in the dialogue between Sage Yājnavalkya and his wife Maitreyī in the *Brihadāranyaka Upanishad*, a well-known scripture of Hinduism. Yājnavalkya said to Maitreyī, "Verily, not for the sake of the wife, my dear, is the wife loved, but she is loved for the sake of the self (which, in its true nature, is one with the Supreme Self)." [1]

A characteristic of each person or object that is dear, is that such a person or object gives joy to those who hold them dear. In other words, anything or anyone that is dear to me must be a source of joy to me. The Self or the *Ātman* is the dearest of all. Therefore, the *Ātman* or the Self is the greatest source of joy. According to *Advaita Vedānta*, the *Ātman* is joy itself.

---

1. See the *Brihadāranyaka Upanishad (2/4/5).*

JOURNEY FROM MANY TO ONE

10

Piercing the Veil of Ignorance

In Chapter 5 it was mentioned that even though we are *Brahman*, ignorance does not allow us to experience our *Brahman*-ness. What is this ignorance? Where is it located? How does it obstruct the experience of our *Brahman*-ness? Is it possible for us to get rid of this ignorance? If it is possible to get rid of ignorance, how can we do it?—Such questions naturally arise in our minds and *Advaita Vedānta* can answer them.

What is ignorance?

The defining characteristic of ignorance is the absence of knowledge. Being opposites, knowledge and ignorance of the same thing cannot coexist anywhere at any given point of time, just as light and darkness cannot coexist at the same place at the same time. If light exists somewhere at a certain time, darkness has to be absent there at that time. So also with knowledge and ignorance.

The ignorance of our *Brahman*-ness and the knowledge or experience of our *Brahman*-ness cannot exist simultaneously. Expressed differently, the veil of ignorance covers the knowledge of our *Brahman*-ness. The very moment the experience or knowledge of *Brahman*-ness comes, the veil of ignorance that covers *Brahman*-ness is destroyed.

Where is ignorance located?

The ignorance of our *Brahman*-ness is located in our minds.

How is ignorance destroyed?

This *mental* ignorance of *Brahman* is destroyed when *mental* knowledge of *Brahman* appears in our minds. According to Srī Rāmakrishna (1836-1886), ignorance of *Brahman* is like a thorn embedded in the flesh of a person. To remove this thorn of ignorance, a second thorn, the thorn of the knowledge of *Brahman*, is used. After removing the first thorn with the second, both are thrown away. What remains is *Brahman*—the one and only Reality— shining beyond the realm of both mind and matter.[1]

Ignorance creates this world; Two kinds of ignorance: *mūlāvidyā* and *tulāvidyā*

Advaita Vedānta says that ignorance of *Brahman* has created this world. Ignorance, which is the opposite of knowledge (*jnāna-virodhī*), is not something negative. It has a positive character (*bhāvarūpa*).

---

1. In Hindu philosophy this analogy is called *kantakoddhārana-nyāya*.

It has two powers: (1) the veiling power (*āvarana-shakti*: *āvarana* = veil/covering, and *shakti* = power) and (2) the power of projection (*vikshepa-shakti*: *vikshepa* = projection). Ignorance has the power to cover or veil the Reality, which is *Brahman*, and also the power to project this world on the veiled or covered Reality.

The expression "absence of knowledge" must not be wrongly interpreted as a state of void or nothingness. In that case it wouldn't have been possible for ignorance to produce something as positive as this world. Even though ignorance is the absence of knowledge, *Advaita Vedānta* insists that ignorance is positive in character. It is not negative. That is why it is capable of creating this world. That such creation is possible through ignorance can be shown by the following analogy:

Let me consider my dream experience. When I fall asleep and start dreaming, I am no longer aware of the world that I experience during my waking state. In other words, I am ignorant of it at that time. While dreaming, I am in a different world, one created by my own mind.

When I create the dream world, I create "dream time" and "dream space" also. But would it be possible for me to create my dream world had I not first become ignorant of the world that I experience while awake? Obviously not.

So it can safely be said that my *ignorance* about the world that I experience during my waking state, is mainly responsible for the creation of my dream world, which I shall call *the first dream world*.

My ignorance about the world of my waking experience may be called "original ignorance" in the sense that *the first dream world* of mine is originated from it. Then again, while existing in my *first dream world* I may still be ignorant of other things that belong to my *first dream world*. This ignorance may be called "secondary ignorance." As soon as I wake up or become aware of this world of my waking experience, my *first dream world* is annihilated.

Similarly, according to *Advaita Vedānta*, the world experienced by us in our waking state is the creation of our *ignorance* of *Brahman*. This kind of ignorance is called "primal ignorance" (*mūla-avidyā* or *mūlāvidyā*). This world is also like another dream world, which I shall call *the second dream world*. While inside this *second dream world*, we still have various kinds of ignorance such as ignorance of what is happening far away, ignorance about what other individuals think, ignorance about difficult subjects like relativity, quantum mechanics, nuclear physics, calculus, etc. This latter kind of ignorance is called in *Advaita Vedānta*, "relative or secondary ignorance" (*tulāvidyā*).

Our knowledge of *Brahman* awakens us from this *second dream world*. When the knowledge of *Brahman* dawns on us, this *second dream world* is annihilated. Then what remains is *Brahman*—the one and only Reality which is beyond time, space and causation.

We can compare *this second dream world*—the world of our waking state—to a large box. Inside this box there is a smaller box—the world of our *first dream experience.*

When we come out of the smaller box we are still inside the larger box. And if and when we come out of this larger box we arrive at *Brahman*-ness. We arrive at Oneness. This is spiritual enlightenment. This is freedom from all kinds of limitation. This is arriving at "One without a Second" (*Ekam-eva-advitīyam*).

Whose dream world is this larger box? From our point of view, "I" am the dreamer; it is "I" who has dreamt up or created this world. In connection with this, the reader is asked to remember the portion relevant to *Eka-Jīva-Vāda* or *Drishti-Srishti-Vāda* in Chapter 6.[2]

The three kinds of experience—waking, dreaming and dreamless sleep

We have so far discussed only two kinds of experience: (1) the waking experience (*jāgrat*) and (2) the dream experience (*swapna*). *Advaita Vedānta* draws our attention to a third experience. It is the experience of dreamless sleep (*sushupti*).

In dreamless sleep the mind becomes unconscious and defunct. Being inactive, it does not record anything. It does not know what happens during the period of dreamless sleep. Yet the person who has had the dreamless sleep, after

---

2. As an alternative to this idea, *Advaita Vedānta* holds that *Saguna Brahman*, by His *māyā*, created the first being named Hiranyagarbha. Even though a created being, Hiranyagarbha has almost God-like powers. He is Cosmic Intelligence. By *Saguna Brahman*'s will, Hiranyagarbha created this world.

waking up, says, "I slept happily. I didn't know anything."

Since the person's mind was inactive during the dreamless sleep and unable to know anything, who *knows* whether during that sleep the person slept happily and did not know anything? According to *Advaita Vedānta*, it is primal ignorance or *mūlāvidyā* that knows it. How this happens can be explained with an analogy borrowed from voice-mail:

When cell phones are turned off, voicemail is received and collected at the telephone company until the individual cell phones are turned on. Until then the messages remain stored with the telephone company. Only when the individual cell phones are turned on, do the voice messages come to them.

In this analogy the telephone company that receives and stores the voicemail is like primal ignorance or *mūlāvidyā*, and individual minds are like so many cell phones. Only when the minds become conscious and functional, do they receive from *mūlāvidyā* the knowledge of having slept happily, and of not having known anything during their dreamless sleep (*sushupti*).

In this connection another question may arise: Since ignorance and knowledge are opposite to each other, how can *mūlāvidyā* or primal ignorance *know* what happens to the individual minds during *sushupti*?

The answer to this question is that this world experienced during our waking state is the creation of *mūlāvidyā*.

Our bodies, minds, sense organs, etc. also belong to this world, and as such are also the creation of *mūlāvidyā*.

Then again, our minds when conscious can think and know. Since minds, which are unconscious matter, can have awareness with the help of consciousness manifested in them, the *mūlāvidyā*, being the *source* of our minds, must also be capable of having awareness the same way. It is this capacity for awareness of *mūlāvidyā* that enables it to know what happens to individual minds during *sushupti*.[3]

The fourth experience (*turīya*)

When you wake up from the dream of this world, like a drop of water becoming one with the infinite ocean, your ego loses its little individuality and becomes one with infinite *Brahman*. Losing its false and puny individuality it acquires its true identity: *Brahman*-ness. This is called the fourth experience. The Sanskrit counterpart of the word "fourth" is "*turīya*."

Advaita Vedānta says that our experience of dreamless sleep (*sushupti*) is contradicted by our dream experience (*swapna*). Then again, the dream experience is contradicted by our waking experience (*jāgrat*). The waking experience is also finally contradicted by the experience of *Brahman*-ness (*turīya*). This fourth experience is never contradicted by any subsequent experience. This experience is the end

---

3. Consciousness or *Brahman* is the substratum of *mūlāvidyā*. That is why consciousness manifests in *mūlāvidyā*. *Mūlāvidyā* is an *upādhi* of Consciousness or *Brahman*. (For *upādhi* see Chapter 13.)

of our journey—arriving from many to One. This is spiritual enlightenment. This is God-realization.

Please see the diagram depicting these four states on the next page.

The individual ego is the product of ignorance (*mūla-avidyā*)

This world is the product of *mūla-avidyā*. The individual ego, which is part of this world, is also the product of *mūla-avidyā*. Consciousness associated with this ego is called the *Ātman* or the *Jīvātman*. Between the *Jīvātman* and *Brahman* (*Paramātman*) there is a thin veil of ignorance. It is like a cloud that does not allow an individual to see the sun. In this analogy *Brahman* is the sun and the patch of cloud is the ignorance of the individual. When this individual's ignorance is dispelled by the knowledge of *Brahman*, he or she will have the experience of *Brahman*-ness.

A scripture of Hinduism called the *Mundaka Upanishad* uses a beautiful analogy to explain how the *Jīvātman* becomes one with the *Paramātman*. It says that the *Jīvātman* and the *Paramātman* are like two identical birds of beautiful plumage, always united and known by the same name and clinging closely to the same tree (same body). One of them (the *Jīvātman*) eats the tree's sweet fruits (objects of sense pleasure). At first the objects of sense pleasure seem to be sweet and enjoyable, but eventually they taste terribly bitter. The other bird

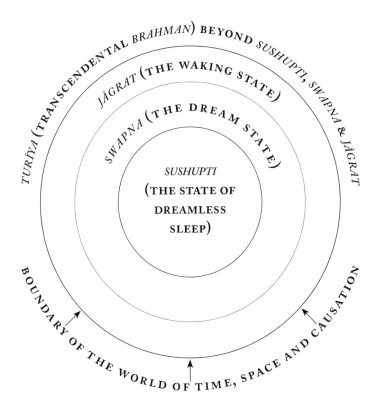

The Four States

(the *Paramātman*) looks on without eating (like a witness, totally disinterested in worldly pleasures).

Seated on the same tree, the *Jīvātman* bird moans (due to its worldly troubles), bewildered by its impotence (helplessness). But when it thinks of the *Paramātman* bird and meditates on how serene it is and how glorious, the *Jīvātman* bird gradually becomes free from grief, as it finally realizes that it has all along been no other than the *Paramātman* bird. (The suffering of the *Jīvātman* is the result of its feeling of impotence. This impotence is destroyed by its knowledge of unity with the *Paramātman*. The grief of the *Jīvātman* is the result of its identification with its body-mind-complex.)

11

Creation and *Advaita Vedānta*: Does the World Really Exist?

When we try to trace the source of anything that exists in this world we end up at some unknown source. For example, if we try to trace the source of a tree we discover that it has come from a seed. Then we realize that the seed must have come from the fruit of another tree, and that tree came from another seed, and so on. If we continue searching backward in time to find the original source of the tree we end up with an unknown source.

We don't know whether the seed came first or the tree. Nevertheless, we realize that there must have been an original source. We also realize that that unknown, original source must have been *uncaused*. Otherwise we encounter the problem of infinite regress.

Our early human ancestors must have thought that this unknown source was extremely mysterious. Therefore, in order to explain this mystery they deified the cause. Some obviously thought that there were as many uncaused unknown sources as there were objects and living beings in the world.

The idea of many gods may have originated in this way.

In the ancient mythologies of India, Rome and Greece we read about many gods and goddesses—the god of the waters (Hindu: *Varuna*; Roman: Neptune), the goddess of wisdom (Greek: Athena), the god of fire (Hindu: *Agni*), the god of the winds (Hindu: *Vāyu*), etc.

Other thinkers thought that there was only one uncaused, unknown source from which the entire world came into existence. According to the latter group of thinkers, there is only one God—God the Almighty. It is this God who has created this world just by His thought. For example, according to the Bible, God said, "Let there be light; and there was light." In other words, whatever God said, happened.

Speaking is no other than thinking aloud. Therefore, we can safely say that according to that approach, whatever God thought came into existence, such as this manifold universe.

Nāsadīya Sukta

In the *Rigveda*, the most ancient scripture of Hinduism, there is a wonderful hymn called the *Nāsadīya Sukta*.[1] Some Western scholars call this the *Creation Hymn*. Since this hymn or *sukta* starts with the compound word *Nāsad*, Hindu scholars call it *Nāsadīya Sukta*. The hymn is so beautiful, so poetic, and so deeply philosophical that I cannot resist the temptation of quoting its English translation below for the readers.

---

1. The *Rigveda*: 10th *Mandala,* 11th *Anuvāka*, hymn 1.

II DOES THE WORLD REALLY EXIST?

Nāsadīya Sukta (Creation Hymn)

Not non-existent was it nor existent was it at that time;
There was not atmosphere nor the heavens which are beyond.
What existed? Where? In whose care?
Water was it? An abyss unfathomable?
Neither mortal was there nor immortal then;
Not of night, of day was there distinction:
"That" alone breathed windless through inherent power.
Other than "That" there was naught else.
Darkness it was, by darkness hidden in the beginning: an
      undistinguished sea was all this.
The germ of all things which was enveloped in void,
"That" alone through the power of brooding thought was born.
Upon "That"' in the beginning arose desire, which was the first
      offshoot of that thought.
This desire sages found out to be the link between the existent and the
      non-existent, after searching with the wisdom in their heart.
Straight across was extended their line of vision: was "That"
      below, was "That" above?
Seed-placers there were, powers there were: potential energy
      below, impulse above.
Who, after all, knows?
Who here will declare whence it arose, whence this world?
Subsequent are the gods to the creation of this world.
Who then, knows whence it came into being?
This world—whence it came into being, whether it was made
      or whether not—
He who is the overseer in the highest heavens surely knows—
      or perhaps He knows not.[2]

---

2. Translated and annotated by Dr. Walter H. Maurer, *Pinnacles of India's Past; Selections from the Rig-Veda.* John Benjamins Publishing Company, Amsterdam/Philadelphia, 1986, pp. 283-84.

In this hymn doubts are raised in the last stanza about the *real* creation of this world. The "overseer in the highest heavens" is *Īshvara/Saguna Brahman* or God, the creator. He is all-knowing. He must know if the world has been created. If He does not know, then it may mean that from His point of view no world has really been created. For what is not really there, the question of knowing its existence cannot arise. Therefore, it does not contradict *Īshvara's* omniscience.

The world has not *really* been created

That *Saguna Brahman* has not *really* created this world is the view of *Advaita Vedānta* as well. According to *Advaita Vedānta*, the world is an illusion only. For the time being it appears to be real, but ultimately it is not real.

This view is also supported by a statement in the *Brihadāranyaka Upanishad* (Verse: 2/5/19), which says, "God by His magical power has become this manifold universe" (*Indro māyābhih pururūpa īyate*).

Let us suppose that a magician has cast a hypnotic spell on his audience. By hypnotic suggestion he creates an apple tree. Under the spell of the magician's hypnotic power the audience will see the apple tree. But the magician will not see it, since he is not under the spell of his own hypnotic power. Similarly, *Īshvara* or *Saguna Brahman* has created this world by His power of magic (*māyā*). Therefore, from *Īshvara's* point of view, this world has no real existence. It was never really created.

From a different perspective, *Saguna Brahman* or *Īshvara* exists for us as long as we are ignorant of *Nirguna Brahman*. When this ignorance is gone, its product, the world, is annihilated; and along with the world we as individuals also cease to exist. Losing our puny individualities we regain our real identity, which is "*Brahman*-ness."

The views of two well-known philosophers of the *Advaita Vedānta* school regarding creation

Now I would like to introduce the readers to two great, saintly philosophers of the *Advaita Vedānta* school and their views about the creation of this world.

Gaudapāda (circa 6th century A.D.) and his *Ajāta-Vāda*. According to Rāmabhadra Dīkshita, Gaudapāda was a disciple of Katanjali. One of the most renowned philosophers of the *Advaita Vedānta* school, Gaudapāda is the author of the famous *Māndūkya-kārikā*, a commentary on the *Māndūkya Upanishad*. The *Māndūkya Upanishad* belongs to the *Atharva Veda*.

Gaudapāda's name is specially associated with the theory known as *Ajāta-vāda* or *Ajāti-vāda*. This theory may also be called the theory of non-origination. According to *Ajāta-vāda*, the perceptual world in which we exist was never created. This theory completely rejects all causality. It does not accept that there is any cause or source of this perceptual world.

This means that in reality nothing is born and nothing dies. There is no birth, no death, no growth, and no decay—in short, no change whatsoever. There is neither bondage nor liberation. Nothing exists except *Brahman*, the one and only Reality.

Due to ignorance (*ajñāna*) about *Brahman* the world *appears* to exist only in the minds of the ignorant (*ajñānī*). When one experiences the Self as one with *Brahman*, the illusion of the world is annihilated. Then what remains is only *Brahman*—the Reality—a state of Eternity (*Sat*), Consciousness (*Chit*) and perpetual Bliss (*Ānandam*). [Please read about the behavior of the *jīvanmuktas* as described at the end of Chapter 3.]

View of Shankarāchārya (circa 6th or 7th century A.D.) Among the saintly philosophers of the *Advaita Vedānta* school, Shankarāchārya is the best known. He lived for only thirty-two years. He was extraordinarily brilliant and also had the experience of *Brahman*. His guru was Govinda Bhagavadpāda.

As far as is known, his *guru*, although a spiritually enlightened soul, was not a renowned scholar of *Advaita Vedānta*. If Shankarāchārya's *guru*, Govinda Bhagavadpāda, was the same Govinda Bhagavadpāda who belonged to the *Raseswara* tradition and who wrote the book on chemistry entitled *Rasahridaya*, then he must have attained spiritual enlightenment using certain chemicals. But there is controversy among scholars about this. The great *advaitist* philosopher Gaudapāda was the *guru* of Govinda Bhagavadpāda.

Shankarāchārya was a prolific author. Within the short span of his life he authored thirty books, including his monumental commentaries on the *Brahmasūtra*s, the *Bhagavad Gītā*, and twelve Upanishads: *Īsha, Kena, Katha, Prashna, Mundaka, Māndūkya, Taittirīya, Aitareya, Chhāndogya, Brihadāranyaka, Shvetāshvatara* and *Nrisimha Pūrvatāpanīya*. Among his other books, *Viveka Chudāmani* and *Aparokshānubhūti* are quite popular.

According to Shankarāchārya, the world exists for a person as long as he or she has not experienced *Brahman*. Only when one experiences *Brahman* does the world become illusory.

Three kinds of existence (*sattā*) recognized by Shankarāchārya

Shankarāchārya recognizes three kinds of existence (*sattā*): (1) empirical existence (*vyāvahārika sattā*), (2) apparent existence (*prātibhāsika sattā*) and (3) ultimate existence (*pāramārthika sattā*). He recognizes the empirical existence of this world, but not its ultimate existence. Only *Brahman* has "ultimate existence." Compared to *Brahman* this world has "empirical existence" only.

Sometimes due to an optical error a rope or a deep, narrow crack in the ground may appear to be a snake. The perception of this snake is a perfect example of "apparent existence." As long as the optical illusion lasts the snake *appears* to exist. When the optical error is gone, the apparent existence of the snake is contradicted by the empirical existence of the rope or the crack in the ground.

Ultimate existence or *pāramārthika sattā* cannot be contradicted by any other existence, such as *vyāvahārika sattā* (empirical existence) and *prātibhāsika sattā* (apparent existence). On the other hand, *pāramārthika sattā* contradicts both *vyāvahārika sattā* and *prātibhāsika sattā*.

According to Shankarāchārya, the empirical existence of this world is contradicted only by the ultimate existence of *Brahman*. However, this world "for the time being" is real and has to be treated as such until we have attained the knowledge of *Brahman*. Until the knowledge of *Brahman* has dawned on us, we do not have the right to dismiss the world as an illusion.

This, however, must not give us the impression that Shankarāchārya does not accept Gaudapāda's *Ajātavāda*. In fact, Shankarāchārya's acceptance of the *vyāvahārika* existence (empirical existence) of this world was not his final say. His favorite analogy of the snake being seen in a rope due to an optical illusion makes this idea clear. In this analogy the reality is the rope or *Brahman*. The snake is a superimposition of the world on the reality, which in this particular case is represented by the rope. This superimposition is due to the viewer's ignorance of the existence of the rope.

As long as this ignorance lasts, the viewer will continue seeing the snake. When the viewer's ignorance is gone, the rope will appear and the superimposed snake will be gone forever. Is it to be supposed then that the superimposed snake was *really* there as long as the viewer's ignorance lasted? The answer is "No." Even when the viewer was seeing the snake, it was *never* really there. In other words, the world was never really there even when it appeared to exist for the time being. This is *Ajāta-Vāda*.

Therefore, this world is only an apparent transformation (*vivarta*) of *Brahman*. It is not a real transformation (*parināma*). When milk becomes transformed into yoghurt it is a case of real transformation or *parināma*. When a rope appears to be a snake because of an optical error, it is an instance of apparent transformation or *vivarta*.

If we have to express Shankarāchārya's view of the world in one sentence, then that sentence is: "*Brahman* alone is real, this world is a *lie* (*mithyā*) and the *Jīvātman* is no other than *Brahman*."[3] In this sentence the word *mithyā* or "lie" has a special connotation. It does not mean that it is fantasy, such as "the son of a barren woman" or "a flower that grows high up in the sky." The word *mithyā* means something that has been imagined in *Brahman*.

And yet, as long as ignorance of *Brahman* remains in the mind of an individual, the world appears to be real *for the time being*. When this ignorance is gone, the imaginary world is also gone. Only *Brahman*, the Eternal Reality, remains.

---

3. In Sanskrit: *Brahma satyam jaganmithyā jīvo brahmaiva nāparah.*

JOURNEY FROM MANY TO ONE

12

The Concept of *Māyā* and Creation

The literal meaning of the word *māyā* is *magic*. However, from the point of view of *Advaita Vedānta*, *māyā* and *avidyā* are the same. Just as *avidyā* or ignorance has the power, *as it were*, to hide *Brahman* and project something else, such as the world, on it, so also *māyā*, *as it were*, can cover up *Brahman* and project the world onto it.

Māyā cannot *really* cover the Reality that is *Brahman*. A patch of cloud can never cover the sun. It only covers the eyes of those who are looking at the sun. In the same way *māyā* covers our *knowing ability* and thus obstructs our knowledge of *Brahman*.

As long as our ignorance of *Brahman* lasts, the world *must* appear to be real to us. So it is natural for us to ask how and when this world of ours was created. *Advaita Vedānta* says that there are two answers to this. The first answer is that this world is *our* dream. We have dreamt up this world. This is *Ekajīva-vāda*. The second answer is that this world is the product of *Saguna Brahman*'s power of magic (*māyā*).

Saguna Brahman has used His *māyā* or magical power to create this world which is unreal like our dream worlds. The *Taittirīya Upanishad* says that after creating the world (using His magical power or *māyā*) He (*Paramātman*) entered into it. (*Tat-sristvā tadevānuprāvishat—Taittirīya Upanishad* 2/6.) It is very much like us creating our individual dream worlds and entering into them. But the difference is that due to our ignorance our dream worlds seem to be real to us. *Saguna Brahman*, however, does not have that kind of ignorance. In one sense, we, the individuals living in this world, are like so many "dream persons" existing in *Saguna Brahman's* conjured up world.

Since we are posited in the domain of *māyā*, looking through the veil of *māyā*, from our point of view *Nirguna Brahman* appears to be *Saguna Brahman*. In reality *Saguna Brahman* is no other than *Nirguna Brahman*.

But we have learnt from Chapter 2 that *Nirguna Brahman* is a non-doer. Therefore, the question arises, "How is it possible for *Nirguna Brahman*, in the garb of *Saguna Brahman*, to create anything, such as this world?"

This question can be answered by drawing the reader's attention to the fact that this world, from the point of view of *Nirguna Brahman*, is not real. It does not exist for *Nirguna Brahman*. Therefore, *Nirguna Brahman* is neither a doer nor a creator.

From *our* point of view, however, *Saguna Brahman*, or *Īshvara*, is the Reality. It is *Saguna Brahman* who has by his *māyā* conjured up this world, which is real to us. Therefore, He alone is the creator and sustainer of this world.[1]

How did *Saguna Brahman* create this world? Does *Advaita Vedānta* have anything to say about this? According to *Advaita Vedānta*, there are two concepts of creation based on the reliable testimony of the scriptures.

First concept of creation

Saguna Brahman first created the element *ākāsha*, (a kind of extremely fine matter or the "sky element"). *Ākāsha* gradually underwent a process of evolution. From *ākāsha* came the element *vāyu* (a fine gaseous substance or the "air element"). From *vāyu* came the element *agni* (an extremely subtle energy or intense heat, also called the "fire element"). From *agni* came the element *ap* (an extremely subtle liquid; it is also called the "water element"). From *ap* came the element *prithivī* (extremely fine solid matter; it is also called the "earth element").[2]

Something that has come into being is called a *bhūta* in Sanskrit. Therefore, these five manifested elements are called *bhūtas*. These elements are extremely subtle. The

1. According to *Advaita Vedānta*, *Saguna Brahman* or *Īshvara* never sleeps or dreams. Yet, for the easier understanding of the readers, I have occasionally been comparing the world conjured up by *Saguna Brahman* to our dream worlds.
2. It is interesting to note that the way today's astrophysicists talk about creation is quite similar to the above process of evolution. In modern scientific terms *ākāsha* could be called dark matter; *agni* could be compared to dark energy; and *ap* could be compared the "lumpy soup" talked about by modern scientists.

Sanskrit counterparts of the words *five* and *subtle* are respectively *pancha* and *sūkshma*. Therefore, these five subtle elements are called *pancha sūkshma-bhūtas*.

These five subtle elements then mingle together in five different ways to produce the five gross (*sthūla*) elements. It is like the subtle presence of the future banyan tree in a seed becoming a full grown banyan tree. These five gross elements are called *pancha sthūla-bhūtas*. The process of mixing the five subtle elements to produce the five gross elements is called *panchīkarana*. The process of such mixing is given below:

The *panchīkarana* process

1/2 subtle *ākāsha* + 1/8 subtle *vāyu* + 1/8 subtle *agni* + 1/8 subtle *ap* + 1/8 subtle *prithivī* produce the "gross" *ākāsha* element.

1/2 subtle *vāyu* + 1/8 subtle *ākāsha* + 1/8 subtle *agni* + 1/8 subtle *ap* + 1/8 subtle *prithivī* produce the "gross" *vāyu* element.

1/2 subtle *agni* + 1/8 subtle *ākāsha* + 1/8 subtle *vāyu* + 1/8 subtle *ap* + 1/8 subtle *prithivī* produce the "gross" *agni* element.

1/2 subtle *ap* + 1/8 subtle *ākāsha* + 1/8 subtle *vāyu* + 1/8 subtle *agni* + 1/8 subtle *prithivī* produce the "gross" *ap* element.

1/2 subtle *prithivī* + 1/8 subtle *ākāsha* + 1/8 subtle *vāyu* + 1/8 subtle *agni* + 1/8 subtle *ap* produce the "gross"

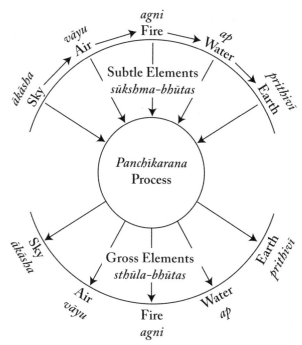

**The Evolution of the Gross Elements
from the Subtle Elements**

prithivī element.

The subtle bodies of humans as well as other living beings are made of the five subtle elements, and the gross body and all the gross objects of nature arise from the mixture of the five gross elements.

Second concept of creation

The *Kathopanishad* (verse 2/3/2, first line) says: "Whatever there is—such as the whole universe—*comes out of*

Brahman and keeps on vibrating."[3] In other words, the cause of this universe is *Brahman*. All objects, living or non-living, are vibrating, but obviously not at the same frequency. Had they been vibrating at the same frequency they would all be the same object. Had they not vibrated at all they would be no different from *Brahman*.

This supposition is borne out by the fact that *Brahman* does not vibrate, only created objects that have come out of *Brahman* do. This also indicates that there must be some direct connection between creation and vibration. We can therefore safely suppose that, due to different frequencies of vibration, *Brahman appears* to have become all the different objects of this universe, whether living or non-living.

Strangely enough, this concept is very similar to the recent concept of scientists that the vibrations of superstring, membrane and D-Brane have given rise to this manifold universe.

More about *māyā*

According to *Advaita Vedānta*, *māyā* has an unknown beginning, but it does have an end. This can be explained by our dream experience. The dream world, which is not real, is created by our minds almost magically. But in order to create the dream world, our minds first have to be

---

3. This means that the whole universe has come out of *Brahman* and is vibrating. This verse in Sanskrit is: *"Yadidang kincha jagat sarvang prāna ejati nihsritam"*—*Kathopanishad* 2/3/2 (first line).

ignorant of the existence of the world that we experience during our waking state. This *ignorance* is comparable to *māyā*. This ignorance is the magical power that creates the dream world along with "dream time" and "dream space."

While in the dream world, it is not possible for us to know *when* the dream world started. In other words, it has an unknown beginning. As soon as we wake up our dream world is annihilated. The dream world is annihilated by our waking experience or the awareness of the world experienced by us during our waking state.

It is not possible for us to know *māyā*

In any act of knowing, the "knower" and "the object known" have to be separate from each other. They cannot be the same. In order for us to know *māyā*, it has to be separate from us. Individuals like us are the products of *māyā* and we are all posited within the domain of *māyā*. *Māyā* and we individuals are not separate from each other, just as chocolate and a bear-shaped chocolate candy are not different from each other.

As we are identical with *māyā*, we cannot know *māyā*. For this reason, *māyā* is not only *unknowable*; it is inexplicable as well (*anirvachanīya*).

Does *māyā* exist?

In answer to this question *Advaita Vedānta* says, "We can't say that *māyā* exists, nor can we say that *māyā* does

113

not exist. For all practical purposes we must admit that *māyā* must exist. If we don't accept *māyā's* existence then we cannot explain the existence of this world. Then again, when we realize our *Brahman*-ness *māyā* disappears. Therefore, we can neither say that *māyā* exists, nor can we say that *māyā* doesn't exist. *Māyā* is inexplicable."

There is an interesting story to explain this. It seems that a well-known gangster once killed a person on a nearly empty street. A man from the porch of a nearby house witnessed the murder. Immediately after the murder the police came and arrested the gangster. Since there were no witnesses other than the man on the porch, the police told him that he must come to the court and be the prime witness to testify against the gangster.

At midnight the witness got a phone call from an unknown person who said, "If you go to court and testify against our leader you're a dead man!" As a result, this man was in a great dilemma. He could neither disobey the police nor could he ignore the threat to his life.

Nevertheless, when the murder case went to court he had to be present there. When the judge asked him, "Did you see the accused commit the murder?" the witness replied, "Your honor, I can neither say 'Yes' nor can I say 'No'."

The judge had studied logic; he knew the law of excluded middle. So he said to the man, "What you say doesn't make any sense. It goes against logic. You must be able to say either 'Yes' or 'No!'"

The man responded, "Your honor, to prove that I'm right would you please permit me to ask you a question?"

The judge replied, "Yes, go ahead and ask your question."

The man asked the judge, "Your honor, do you *still* beat your wife?"

Now the judge was in trouble. Had he replied, "No," it would mean that he used to beat his wife and now he doesn't beat her anymore. On the other hand, had he replied, "Yes," that would have been even worse. So it was proved that the judge also was not able to say either "Yes" or "No."

Similarly, since *māyā* has only *empirical* existence and no *ultimate* existence, one cannot say that *māyā* exists, nor can one say that it doesn't exist.

Vidyā māyā and *avidyā māyā*

Since we exist in the domain of *māyā*, is it ever possible for us to get rid of *māyā*? *Advaita Vedānta* assures us that it is possible. In order to go beyond *māyā* we have to take the help of *māyā* itself. According to a popular saying in India, if we fall to the ground, we have to push against the ground to get up again. The ground itself will help us to get up.

There is another beautiful analogy in *Advaita Vedānta* to explain this: Suppose I am extremely scared of tigers. While dreaming I suddenly see a tiger about to jump on me. This frightens me so much that I immediately wake up. When I wake up, both my dream world and the dream tiger are gone. The tiger belonged to my dream world. Nevertheless, it dissolved my entire dream world.

Srī Rāmakrishna used to say, "*Māyā* consists of two parts. One part hinders the knowledge of *Brahman*; the other part helps to get rid of *māyā*. The first part is *avidyā-māyā* or the '*māyā* of ignorance' and the second part is *vidyā-māyā* or the '*māyā* of knowledge.'" *Vidyā-māyā* is like the dream tiger. This includes the various religious scriptures, all the concepts of God and Divine Incarnations, various spiritual disciplines, etc., that may help one to go beyond *māyā* and experience one's *Brahman*-ness.

The ideas of *vidyā-māyā* and *avidyā-māyā* also answer questions such as, "According to *Advaita-Vāda*, this world is an illusion. Why then does it appear to be so real to us? Or, how can we go beyond this illusory world?"

13

The Relationship Between *Brahman* and the World

It appears that since *Brahman* is real and the world illusory there cannot be any relationship between *Brahman* and the world. What is the view of *Advaita Vedānta* in this respect?

According to Shankarāchārya, the world has empirical existence but no ultimate existence. As long as it lasts it is real. When the knowledge of *Brahman* is attained, the world becomes illusory, *not before that*. As long as this world appears to exist, it must exist in *Brahman*—the eternal Reality. *Brahman* is like the ever-enduring canvas upon which this transient world-picture has been painted by *Brahman*'s *māyā*.

The three aspects of *Brahman*—*asti, bhāti* and *priya*

According to Shankarāchārya's *Kevalādvaita Vāda*, *Brahman* is the substratum of this world-picture. Had the canvas, which is *Brahman*, not been there, no world-picture could have been painted. In other words, the *existence* of the world-picture is no other than the *existence* of the canvas, which is *Brahman*. We are actually seeing the canvas as the picture. The canvas existing, the picture exists. Therefore, the existence of the world is the existence of *Brahman*.

But we learned in Chapter 1 that *Brahman* and existence are identical, because *Brahman* is True Existence (*Sat*). It is this Existence that is being manifested as the existence of this world. Therefore, the *existence* aspect of this world is *Brahman*. This aspect is called the *asti* aspect of *Brahman*.

Saguna Brahman (God the creator) with the help of His *māyā* becomes this manifold universe or manifests this world. This *manifestation* aspect of *Brahman* as this world is the *bhāti* aspect of *Brahman*.

Then again from Chapter 9 of this book we have learnt that *Ātman/Brahman* is the dearest of all. This *dearness* aspect of *Brahman* is called in Sanskrit the *priya* aspect.

Nāma (name) and *rūpa* (form)

Besides these three aspects of *Brahman*, every manifested object in this world has two additional aspects. They are *nāma* (name) and *rūpa* (form). Thus, every object in creation has all five aspects: *nāma, rūpa, asti, bhāti* and *priya*. Among them *nāma* and *rūpa* relate to this world of māyā, and *asti, bhāti* and *priya* relate to *Brahman*. Being the product of *māyā*, this world of *nāma* and *rūpa* are illusory, but the other three aspects that pertain to

Brahman are eternal.

If we analyze we shall discover that all the objects we know have these five aspects. For example, the object that we call a pot has a name (*nāma*). That *name* is "pot." The round shape of the pot is its *form* (*rūpa*). The pot exists. This existence is its *asti* aspect. The pot is being revealed to us, otherwise we would not be aware of it. This *revelation* or *manifestation* of the pot is its *bhāti* aspect. The pot is dear to those who like the pot. This *dearness* of the pot is its *priya* aspect. [Everything in creation, no matter how ugly or dangerous, is dear to someone. Even an ugly warthog or a venomous cobra must be dear to at least its own mate.]

In short, *Brahman*, which is transcendent, is also immanent in this world. The *asti, bhāti* and *priya* aspects of this creation indicate the immanence of *Brahman*. The world of *nāma* and *rūpa* is only a superimposition on *Brahman* by *māyā*. It is therefore not real.

Four important theories in *Advaita Vedānta*

There are four well-known theories or *vāda*s in *Advaita Vedānta* that explain the relationship between *Brahman*, the world (*jagat*) and the individual being (*jīva*). These theories are (1) the Theory of Reflection (*Pratibimba-Vāda*), (2) the Theory of Appearance (*Ābhāsa-Vāda*), (3) the Theory of Limitation (*Avachchheda-Vāda*) and (4) the Theory of "Perception is Creation" (*Drishti-Srishti-Vāda*).

(1) The Theory of Reflection (*Pratibimba-Vāda*). A sub-school of *Advaita Vedānta* called the *Vivarana* school propounds this theory. Padmapādāchārya and Vivaranāchārya were the two main proponents of this theory. According to this theory, the relationship between *Brahman* and the world (*jagat*) and the individual beings (*jīvas*) is very similar to the relationship between a face and its reflection in a mirror.

In spite of the obvious resemblance, the reflection of the face in the mirror is not exactly like the face. In the reflection the right ear becomes the left ear, the right eye becomes the left eye, and so on. In that sense the reflection of the face is not exactly like the face. While the face is real its reflection is not.

If the mirror is cracked or if its surface is uneven, these defects will show on the reflection, but not on the face itself. In this analogy the face is *Brahman* and the reflection is the world and the individual beings. The reflection not being real, the world and the individual beings are not real. *Brahman* alone is real.

(2) The Theory of Appearance (*Ābhāsa-Vāda*). Vidyāranyaswāmī, Bhāratītīrtha and others favored this theory. According to this theory, the world and individual beings are only appearances on *Brahman*.

(3) The Theory Of Limitation (*Avachchheda-Vāda*). Before I introduce this theory it is necessary to explain the philosophical term *limiting adjunct* (*upādhi*). Suppose that there is a large multifaceted, colorless, transparent crystal on a table. Now if we place a red rose so that it is touching one side of the crystal and then look at the crystal from

the opposite side, the crystal will appear to be red. This redness is not an integral quality of the crystal. The redness manifests in the crystal due to its temporary association with the red rose. As soon as the rose is taken away, the crystal becomes colorless again. The redness that came to the crystal due to its temporary association with the red rose is called an *upādhi* or limiting adjunct of the crystal.

Now let me turn to the Theory of Limitation or *Avachchheda-Vāda*. To understand it, an analogy in regard to the relationship between the space enclosed in an empty pot and the space outside the pot can be very helpful. The pot appears to limit the limitless outer space, since the space inside the pot (*ghatākāsha*) seems to be different from the space outside the pot (*mahākāsha*).

In reality, however, space cannot be divided. In this analogy the space seemingly enclosed by the pot represents the Individual Being or *Ātman*. The space outside the pot represents *Brahman*.

This apparent *limitation* of outer space by the pot is false because the enclosed space or *ghatākāsha* is in reality the same outer space or *mahākāsha*. When the limiting adjunct (*upādhi*) such as the pot is removed, the true unity of both spaces (the *Ātman* and *Brahman*) becomes known.

(4) The Theory of "Perception Is Creation" (Drishti-Srishti-Vāda). According to this theory, seeing is creating. For example, the dream world is created at the very moment when the dreamer sees it. The same thinking is applicable to this world in which we are located. This theory has been explained in Chapter 6. This theory is also called *Eka-Jīva-Vāda*.

Besides these four theories, *Advaita Vedānta* also accepts the following two theories.

(a) *Vivarta-Vāda* (Theory of Apparent Change). In Hindu philosophy, cause is generally of two kinds—(i) material cause (*upādāna-kāranam*: *upādāna* = material, *kāranam* = cause) and (ii) efficient cause (*nimitta-kāranam*). For example, consider an iron ball. In this example the ball is an effect. Its material cause is iron, because iron is the material that was used to make the ball. But the ball could not have been produced without a blacksmith and his tools. Thus the blacksmith and his tools are the efficient cause of the ball.

In regard to the ball, one might say that its material cause, iron, was *really* transformed into the ball. In other words, the material cause was *really* made into the effect. Such transformation is called *parināma* in Sanskrit. There are some schools of Hindu philosophy that maintain that this world is a real transformation or *parināma* of *Brahman*.

According to *Advaita Vedānta*, however, the world is only an *apparent* transformation of *Brahman*. Such apparent transformation is called a *vivarta* in Sanskrit. The theory of such apparent transformation of *Brahman* into the world is called *Vivarta-Vāda*.

A good example of *Vivarta-Vāda* is the case of a rope that appears to have become a snake because of the optical illusion of the observer. In this analogy the rope is *Brahman* and the snake is this world. Such transformation was possible only because the observer was *ignorant* of the rope. This ignorance of the reality of the rope (*Brahman*) is called *māyā*.[1] It is this *māyā* which causes this unreal world to *appear* in *Brahman*.

(b) *Satkārya-Vāda*. *Advaita Vedānta* also holds that something cannot come out of nothing. Based on this view another theory called *Satkārya-Vāda* has been developed. According to this theory, the *effect* prior to its manifestation exists in the *cause* in a latent state.

Let us take for example a marble sculpture of a horse. According to *Satkārya-Vāda*, before its manifestation this horse was already present in the cause. But which cause? As mentioned earlier, there are two kinds of cause—the material cause and the efficient cause. In this particular case the material cause is marble, and the efficient cause is the sculptor and the sculptor's tools, such as the chisel, etc.

It cannot be denied that the horse must have *existed* first in its efficient cause—in the mind of the sculptor. The sculptor first took a huge chunk of marble and mentally visualized the form of the horse in it. Then he started chipping away the portion of the marble that did not belong to the form of the horse. Thus the horse, which

---

1. See Chapter 12 for more discussion on *māyā*.

had already existed in the marble block—its *material cause*—became manifest.

According to *Advaita Vedānta*, this world is only an *appearance* on *Brahman*. However, its apparent existence is real in the sense that this existence is no other than *Brahman's* existence. Therefore, this world was already present in *Brahman* as *existence*.

The analogy of *Brahman* as the movie screen and this world as a movie projected on it can explain this clearly. *Brahman* is like the movie screen on which everything in creation has been projected like a movie. The existence of whatever we watch in the movie depends upon the existence of the movie screen. Thus the existence of this manifold world is no other than *Brahman's* existence. In the technical language of philosophy *Brahman* is the substratum (*adhishthāna*) of this creation.

Other than the above, there is another theory called *Ārambha-Vāda or Asatkārya-Vāda* which is not accepted by *Advaita Vedānta*.

Ārambha-Vāda or Asatkārya-Vāda: There are some schools in Hindu philosophy that do not accept *Satkārya-Vāda*. For example: (1) the *Mīmāmsā* or *Pūrva Mīmāmsā* school, (2) the *Nyāya* school and (3) the *Vaisheshika* school do not accept *Satkārya-Vāda*. These schools hold that the effect is something new produced by the cause. And as such, cause and effect are entirely different from each other. In other words, the effect is non-existent in the cause before its production.

This theory is illustrated in the analogy of yarn and a cloth. Some yarn is woven into a cloth. The cloth was not present in its cause, the yarn. This is called the theory of *Ārambha-Vāda* or *Asatkārya-Vāda*. *Advaita Vedānta* does not accept this theory.

Brahman is both the material cause and the efficient cause of this world

According to *Advaita Vedānta*, *Brahman* is both the material cause and the efficient cause of this world. The analogy of a spider and its web is used to explain this idea. *Brahman* is like a spider that has woven its web. The web represents this world. Just as the spider is both the material cause and the efficient cause of its web, so also *Brahman* is both the material cause and the efficient cause of this world.

JOURNEY FROM MANY TO ONE

14

Can We Know *Brahman* Exhaustively?

We have learnt from Chapter 3 that only a pure mind can know *Brahman*. We have also learnt that a spiritual aspirant can know *Brahman* through *Nirvikalpa Samādhi*. Since *Brahman* is beyond time, space and causation, some sages and saintly scholars say that it is impossible to know *Brahman exhaustively* by the mind, which belongs to the domain of time, space and causation. It can only *indirectly* acquire some knowledge of *Brahman*.

As long as the mind remains, the possibility of its degradation cannot be completely ruled out. The Sage Vashishtha was of the opinion that spiritual liberation cannot be attained as long as the mind remains, no matter how pure it is. As long as the mind exists, there will remain some desire, no matter how noble and good. All desires, good or bad, can be destroyed only when the mind is annihilated. And that can happen only when the cloud of ignorance that seems to cover *Brahman* is destroyed.

When that happens, this world and all the creatures in it are gone forever. As no one is there, the question of knowing *Brahman* cannot arise. *Brahman* alone abides. Nothing else does. Should we then suppose that *Brahman* alone knows *Brahman*? That also is not possible. It is not possible for *Brahman* to know *Brahman* for two reasons:

Firstly, we have learnt from Chapter 2 that action can only take place within time and space. As *Brahman* (*Nirguna Brahman*) is beyond time, space and causation, *Brahman* does not act. Since knowing is action, it is not possible for *Brahman* to know *Brahman*.

Secondly, *Brahman alone* exists. The oneness of *Brahman* cannot accommodate the triad (*triputī*) of knower, knowledge and the object known. So the question of *Brahman* being engaged in any action like *knowing Brahman* cannot arise.

But we may argue, drawing attention to the fact that our mind, which is a single entity, knows itself: Why won't *Brahman* be able to know *Brahman*? The answer is that mind can be partitioned, but *Brahman* is indivisible. (See Chapter 1, subtitle: *Brahman* is indivisible.) So far as the mind is concerned, the ego, which is an idea of the mind, knows the rest of the mind. *Brahman* does not have such division within itself. Therefore the question of *Brahman* knowing *Brahman* does not arise.

Now a student of *Advaita Vedānta* may ask, "If no one can know *Brahman* exhaustively, why should we study *Ad-*

vaita Vedānta?" The answer given is that as we are within the domain of time, space and causation, we experience various kinds of limitation. And every kind of limitation causes suffering. We suffer when we feel limited in our health, wealth, intellect, beauty, fame, etc.

Advaita Vedānta can help us to go beyond suffering by pointing out that in reality we are beyond all kinds of limitation. We are that infinity called *Brahman*. Ignorance of our true identity makes us think that we are limited. We are like the infinite ocean. It is a shame that we think of ourselves as tiny drops of water. *Advaita Vedānta* reminds us of what we truly are. It reminds us of our ocean-ness or *Brahman*-ness. An analogy will make this idea more clear:

Suppose that a person named John has to play the leading role in *Hamlet* by William Shakespeare. During the performance, however, something strange happens to John. He identifies himself completely with the role that he is playing. Even when the play is over, he thinks that he is Hamlet.

When he returns home, his wife says, "John, supper is ready. Come and eat."

"Who is John?" John asks his wife with surprise, "Why are you calling me 'John?' Don't you know that I am Hamlet?"

His perplexed and worried wife then tries to convince John in so many ways that he is not Hamlet. She tells him again and again, " You *are* John, and you have always been John. You should shake off the wrong idea that you are Hamlet!" In this analogy John's wife represents *Advaita Vedānta* and John represents those who have forgotten their true nature.

Swāmī Vivekānanda (1863-1902), who, at the end of the 19th century was the first to preach the message of *Advaita Vedānta* in the West, used to call this process "dehypnotization." Forgetting our *Brahman* nature, we have hypnotized ourselves into thinking that we are puny human beings, subject to disease, decay, death and all other kinds of limitation. To become free from such limitations we have to dehypnotize ourselves by meditating on our *Brahman* nature.

Advaita Vedānta, like John's wife, tries to remind its students that they indeed *are Brahman*, whether they know it or not. Not only that, they have always been *Brahman*, and they will remain so forever! They only have to get rid of their wrong thinking produced by the ignorance of their true nature.

There is a statement in the *Vedas* that says "One who knows *Brahman becomes Brahman* (*Brahmaveda Brahmaiva bhavati*)." In other words, to acquire one's *Brahman* nature one has first to know *Brahman*. This statement, if not correctly understood, may create the false notion that one (the *jīva*) was not *Brahman* before; rather, only after knowing *Brahman* later, does one become *Brahman*. The fact, however, is that all along the *jīva* was *Brahman*.

Only after the removal of the cloud of ignorance that seemingly covers *Brahman* is the *Brahman*-ness of the *jīva* revealed in full splendor.

This idea is explained by the following analogy. Once a king was sailing on the sea in his royal boat. Suddenly a severe storm arose. The boat capsized, but the king and the queen were rescued. Their only child, the baby prince, was unfortunately lost at sea.

Later a childless fisherman found the baby floating in the sea and rescued him with the help of his fishing net. The fisherman thought that God had at last graciously given him a child. Thus, he brought up the prince as his own son. And the prince also thought of himself as the fisherman's son.

When the prince grew to be a young man, he would go to sell fish in the market with his fisherman father. One day the king's minister saw him there. The prince had a rare birthmark on his forehead. Seeing that birthmark, the king's minister suspected that the young man was most probably the missing prince.

After talking to the fisherman, he became convinced that the young man was indeed the prince who had been lost at sea. When the prince heard that news, the wrong notion that he was the fisherman's son was gone and he realized that he was a prince.

It is not that he was the fisherman's son before and then *became* a prince. He realized that he had all along been a prince, even when he considered himself to be the fisherman's son. So also the *jīva* does not *become Brahman*. The *jīva*'s *Brahman*-ness becomes instantly revealed as soon as the *jīva*'s false identity as a human being disappears.

15

We Travel from Lower Truth to Higher Truth

Once I asked a little girl who had lost one of her front teeth, "Where has your tooth gone?"

She replied, "The tooth fairy took away my tooth. When my tooth came out, my daddy told me, 'When you go to bed put the tooth under your pillow. The tooth fairy will come after you fall asleep and take away the tooth. As you are a good girl, she will give you a nice gift.' When I woke up my tooth was gone and there was a dollar under my pillow."

To that little girl the tooth fairy was real. It would be impossible to convince her that the tooth fairy did not exist. To her it was true that the tooth fairy had really come and taken away the tooth, and left the dollar for her.

If challenged, she could have used arguments to prove the truth of the tooth fairy's existence. She could have used the logical methods of perception, inference and reliable testimony to validate that truth. Through "perception" she had come to know that the tooth was gone from under her pillow and the dollar had appeared there. She believed the "testimony" of her father who had told her that the tooth fairy would come, take the tooth away and leave a gift for her. Although she did not see the tooth fairy come, she concluded through "inference" that the tooth fairy must have come.

This is an example of *lower* truth. When the little girl grows up she will know that it was not the tooth fairy, but one of her parents who must have taken the tooth away and left the dollar as a gift for her. This second *higher* truth will replace the first lower truth. This is why Swāmī Vivekānanda said, "We don't travel from error to truth. We travel from lower truth to higher truth."

According to Srī Rāmakrishna (1836-1886), the truth of *Advaita* is the highest of all truths.

As mentioned in Chapter 4, among the six systems of Hindu philosophy the *Vedānta* system alone has as many as twelve branches, one of which is the school of *Advaita Vedānta*. They have been recorded under the sub-heading "Branches of the *Vedānta* system." To give the reader some idea about their different views I am going to mention in brief the views of two schools, other than the school of *Advaita Vedānta*. They are (1) the *Dvaita* school and (2) the *Vishishtādvaita* school.

The Dualistic school of the *Vedānta* system, or the school of *Dvaita-Vāda*, also known as *Svatantrā-svatantra-Vāda*, developed by Madhva,[1] teaches that God (*Saguna Brahman*), individual souls (*jīvas*), and the world (*jagat*) are eternally separate from one another, and they are all real. Even though separate, *jīvas* form a part of *Brahman*.

Āchārya Srī Madhva (1238 – 1317)

In relation to God the *jīva* is like an atom (*anu*). God is independent, but the *jīva* and the world are

---

1. Also known as *Ānandatīrtha*.

not. They are dependent on God. God, according to this school, is the supreme deity Vishnu, who is the creator, sustainer and destroyer of this world. He has infinite virtues. He is omnipresent, omniscient and omnipotent. Whenever the need arises, He descends on earth as a Divine Incarnation. He is the efficient cause of this world, while Mother Nature or *prakriti* is its material cause.

This school believes in post-mortem liberation (*moksha/mukti*) only. It does not believe in *jīvanmukti* (liberation here and now). A person who has gone through rigorous ethical and moral disciplines, followed by right knowledge, right action, non-attachment, worship and devotional meditation (*upāsanā*) on the Personal God (Vishnu), becomes fit for *moksha* (liberation) through God's loving grace.

In ascending order, this school believes in four levels of *moksha*: (1) *sālokya*, (2) *sāmīpya*, (3) *sārūpya* and (4) *sāyujya*. Depending upon its level of spiritual progress, the departed soul may achieve any one of the four kinds of *moksha*.

In *sālokya-mukti* the departed soul goes to *Ishta-loka* (the abode of the Personal God, such as the abode of Vishnu) and stays there blissfully enjoying His presence. In *sāmīpya-mukti* the departed soul enjoys the bliss of extreme proximity to the Personal God. In *sārūpya-mukti* the departed soul acquires the form of the Personal God and enjoys intense bliss. In *sāyujya-mukti* the departed

136

soul becomes blissfully absorbed in the Personal God.

The school of Qualified Non-Dualism, or *Vishishtādvaita-Vāda*, is also a school of theism.[2] Its main exponent was Rāmānuja. According to this school, there are three ultimate realities—*Īshvara* (*Saguna Brahman*), *chit* (*jīva*) and *achit* (Mother Nature or *prakriti* that evolves as this material universe).

Srī Rāmānuja (1077 – 1157)

---

2. Theism is the belief in the existence of a creator God.

They exist in an inseparable relationship. *Chit* and *achit*, however, are dependent upon *Īshvara*, who is independent. *Chit* and *achit* are included in *Īshvara* as constituent parts. Such separation or distinction within *Īshvara* is called *svagata-bheda* (See Chapter 1, sub-heading: *Brahman* is Indivisible).

According to this school, *Īshvara* is the Supreme Being (*Purushottama*), Vishnu. *Īshvara* is the repository of infinite virtues. He is omnipotent, omniscient, self-existent, and of the nature of consciousness. In relation to *Īshvara*, the *jīva* is like an atom (*anu*) and is subservient to Him. *Īshvara* is both the efficient and the material cause of this world.

According to this school, *upāsanā* consists of ritualistic worship, devotional practices and various kinds of meditation on God. The God-experience of an individual is possible only through the grace of God. A person can have *moksha* or liberation only after the person's death. *Moksha* means living blissfully in *Vaikuntha* (the abode of Vishnu). Like *Dvaita-Vāda* this school also does not accept the idea of *jīvanmukti*.

Persons who have attained *moksha* live blissfully in *Vaikuntha* in spiritual bodies in the presence of God. They acquire many divine powers such as omniscience, but unlike God they cannot create, sustain or dissolve the world. In spite of their exalted state they remain subservient to God.

According to this school, liberation cannot be attained here and now by experiencing one's *Brahman*-ness (*Ātma-*

jnāna) as maintained by the *Advaita Vedānta* school. This school also says that *bhakti-yoga* (the path of devotion) is the only means of God-realization. *Karma-yoga* (the path of right action) and *jnāna-yoga* (the path of philosophical inquiry) are only aids to *bhakti-yoga*.

In spite of the different views held by these schools, *Advaita Vedānta* is not in *real* conflict with any of them. From the viewpoint of *Advaita Vedānta* they are only so many lower truths.

Shankarāchārya, one of the greatest exponents of *Advaita Vedānta*, is of the view that *upāsanā* (worship) is useful for the purification of mind. In the initial stage, *bhakti-yoga* can be helpful. For this reason Shankarāchārya himself wrote many devotional hymns in adoration of various deities representing *Īshvara* or *Saguna Brahman*. The mind, thus purified through devotional practices, is to be used to practice *jnāna-yoga*. Through *shravana, manana* and *nididhyāsana*, as prescribed by *jnāna-yoga*, one will experience *Brahman*. This is spiritual enlightenment. This is liberation. Such liberation can be had even when one is still alive here on earth. This is called *jīvan-mukti*.[3] A person who attains *jīvan-mukti* is called a *jīvanmukta*. After death a *jīvanmukta* becomes one with *Brahman*. This is called *videha-mukti*.

There is yet another concept about liberation in *Advaita Vedānta*, called *krama-mukti* or *avāntara-mukti*

---

3. See *jīvanmukta* in Chapter 3, sub-heading: Who is a *jīvanmukta*?.

(liberation by stages). According to this concept, a person who has intensely meditated on *Saguna Brahman* using the sacred sound symbol of God, *Aum,* or other prescribed methods of meditation such as *dahara-vidyā*, goes after death to *Brahma-Loka* (the realm of *Saguna Brahman*). There the aspirant attains the knowledge of *Nirguna Brahman* under the guidance of a spiritually exalted being (*Hiranyagarbha*). When the entire universe is dissolved at the end of the *kalpa* (a long periodic cycle of creation and dissolution) the person becomes one with *Nirguna Brahman* and is not born again. This kind of liberation is called *krama-mukti* or *avāntara-mukti.*

Before I end this chapter, I feel it necessary to tell the reader what *dahara-vidyā* means. Many cannot comprehend the transcendental *Nirguna Brahman*. Scriptures such as the *Chhāndogya Upanishad* instruct one to worship and meditate on *Brahman* as It appears in space and time, an entity endowed with certain attributes and dwelling in the human heart. The knowledge of this kind of worship is *dahara-vidyā*. After death the worshipper goes to the realm of *Saguna Brahman* (*Brahma-Loka*) and ultimately attains the knowledge of *Nirguna Brahman* under the guidance of Hiranyagarbha (the highest created being through whom *Saguna Brahman* projects this world).

Why Hinduism Contains Some of the World's Oldest Religio-Philosophical Systems

Hinduism, the oldest of all major religions, belongs to the oldest living civilization of this planet.[1] The difference between a young civilization and an old civilization is comparable to the difference between the young and the elderly.

The young usually have a lot of physical vigor and intelligence, which no matter how keen, tends to be superficial. It has expanse but not much depth.

On the other hand, the elderly do not have their youthful vigor anymore. Having crossed the storms of passion they have acquired relatively calm and serene minds and are now capable of deep and unbiased thinking. Relieved of the intellectual arrogance of their youth, they become fit for acquiring "wisdom," that rare and precious commodity which is the outcome of their many years of ex-

1. *Information Please Almanac* (Boston: Houghton Mifflin Company, 1993), 411.

perience. Their wisdom enables them to become broad-minded, forgiving, and tolerant of other people's views.

In ancient times, when civilization was very young, all human ancestors lived in tribal societies. The idea of nationhood came much later. A tribal society didn't have as many moral and ethical injunctions and prohibitions as we have today. Thus it was a much freer society. At the same time, it had extreme rigidity in religious thinking.

For example, let us consider a typical tribal society of the prehistoric period. Let us suppose that the tribe lived on a volcanic island cut off from the rest of humanity. Its world was one of ignorance, mystery, magic, superstition and fear. The strongest man in the tribe became the chief. He was also the best hunter and warrior. As in any animal pack, this tribe also maintained a strict pecking order, the chief being at the top of the social ladder. The second most powerful member of the tribe was the medicine man cum priest, imagined to possess great magical power. Even the chief treated him with awe.

The island had a dormant volcano that erupted periodically spewing out lava and causing a lot of suffering to the tribe. The medicine man had determined that a deity must live inside that volcano. Judging by the great devastating power of the volcano, he had concluded that it must be an enormously strong *male* deity. As with any dormant volcano, when pressure would build up inside, the volcano erupted and lava started flowing out of its crater until the pressure was relieved. Then it became dormant again for some years.

Once in the past, when pressure had built up inside the volcano, lava started pouring out of its crater. Terrified people went to the medicine man seeking his advice. He said that the volcano god had become angry, and to appease him a young woman had to be sacrificed. Then one hapless young woman was forcibly thrown into the red-hot, flowing lava as an offering to the deity. Some days later when the lava flow stopped on its own, the medicine man claimed all the credit for this. Had anyone in that tribe questioned or doubted the existence of that so called volcano god, he most probably would have been killed. Such lack of tolerance caused by extreme rigidity in religious thinking is a common characteristic of people belonging to younger civilizations.

The civilization in India is the oldest living civilization of the world. The only other comparable ancient civilization that's still alive today is China. The ancient Egyptian civilization has long ago gone out of existence. So also has the relatively younger Aegean civilization. The Greeks, who destroyed the Aegean civilization and later built their own, appeared on the stage only around 1500 B.C.

As the civilization in India grew older it acquired wisdom. Along with that wisdom came broadmindedness and the spirit of tolerance to accept newer religious and metaphysical thoughts. That's why the word "blasphemy" is not to be found anywhere in Hindu religious thought.

In Hinduism any sincere and rational question can be raised. As a result, over the past several thousand years, all possible questions have been asked. And numerous Hindu thinkers, who appeared on the stage at different periods of time, have provided appropriate answers to those questions. Those questions and answers form the foundation of Hindu philosophy.

Aside from that, not having a known founder also has been a blessing to Hinduism. Had it been a religion with a specific founder, it would have been hard for Hinduism to undergo the kind of evolution it has had over the past many thousand years. Various saintly souls and philosophers at different times have appeared on the stage, played their individual roles, and enriched Hinduism with their teachings. They have reformed and revitalized this religion and made it relevant to the changing times and people. This would not have been possible had Hinduism had a single known founder.

17

The Antiquity of *Advaita Vedānta* and its Well-Known Teachers

One may naturally wonder when *Advaita Vedānta* originated. Scholars, both Western and Indian, have varying views about this. But it is generally accepted that the idea of *Advaita* first dawned in the Vedic period when, among other things, the *Upanishadic* truths were revealed to the Hindu sages.

But how old are the *Vedas*, which include the *Upanishad*s? Bālgangādhar Tilak, after thorough research, concluded that the *Vedas* were compiled no later than 4,000 B.C. But most Hindus generally believe that the *Vedas* were compiled by Krishna-dvaipāyana Vyāsa, also known as Bādarāyana, at the time of the Kurukshetra War. According to the great Hindu epic *Mahābhārata*, the Kurukshetra War took place more than 5,000 years ago. Therefore, following these viewpoints Advaitic thoughts must be at least more than 5,000 years old.

Among the most illustrious teachers of the *Advaita*

tradition we must name Vyāsa first. Starting with him, a chronological list of names of famous teachers of *Advaita Vedānta* is given below:

(1) Bādarāyana Vyāsa (3,000 B.C.): Vyāsa was the son of Sage Parāshara. He authored the famous book *Brahmasūtra*, also known as the *Vedānta-darshanam*. Later Hindu philosophers, such as Shankarāchārya, Bhāskarāchārya, Shrīkantha, Rāmānujāchārya, Nimbārka, Vallabhāchārya, Madhvāchārya, Vijnānabhikshu, Baladev Vidyābhushan and Panchānan Tarkaratna, have written many commentaries on this book.

(2) Kāshakritsna (B.C.): There is reference to him in Vyāsa's *Brahmasūtra*. So some scholars believe he predated Vyasa. Other scholars believe he was a contemporary of Vyāsa. (*Brahmasūtra:* aphorism # 1/4/22).

(3) Upavarsha (B.C.): He is famous for writing commentaries on the *Pūrva-mīmāmsā* and *Uttara-mīmāmsā* systems of philosophy. Some scholars think that Shankarāchārya's commentary on the *Brahmasūtra* was influenced by Upavarsha's commentaries on the *Pūrva-mīmāmsā* and *Uttara-mīmāmsā* systems.

(4) Brahmanandī (B.C.): He is famous for writing the commentary *Vākya* on the *Chhāndogya Upanishad.*

(5) Dravidāchārya (B.C.): He wrote a commentary on Brahmanandī's famous commentary *Vākya*, as mentioned above.

(6) Gaudapāda (6th century A.D.): His famous book is *Māndūkyakārikā*, a commentary on the *Māndūkyopanishad*. He is famous as the founder of *Ajātavāda*. Shankarāchārya wrote a commentary on *Māndūkyakārikā*, at the end of which he gave his heart-felt tribute and salutation to Gaudapāda.

Gaudapāda was the guru of Shankarāchārya's guru, Govinda Bhagavadpāda.

(7) Shankarāchārya (7th century A.D.): He was born in Kalady in the state of Kerala in South India. There are differences of opinion about when he lived. It is generally thought that he lived in the 7th century A.D. But according to the book *Vedānta Darshaner Itihās* (a history of *Vedānta* Philosophy) by Prajnānānanda Sarasvatī, he was born in 44 B.C. He lived for only 32 years.

A paragon of *Advaita Vedānta*, he authored at least thirty books. Included among them are his wonderful commentaries on the *Brahmasūtra*s (known as the *Sharīraka Bhāshya*), twelve principal *Upanishad*s, the *Bhagavad Gītā* and the *Vishnu-sahasra-nāma*. The other important books authored by him are: *Sanatsujātīya Bhāshya* (*bhāshya* = commentary), *Lalitātrishatī Bhāshya*, *Viveka Chudāmani*, *Upadesha Sāhasrī*, *Aparokshānubhūti*, *Shatashlokī*, *Dashashlokī*, *Sarva-Vedānta-Siddhāntasāra-Sangraha*, *Vākyasudhā*, *Panchīkarana*, *Drik Darshana Viveka*, *Dakshināmūrti Stotra* (*stotra* = hymn), *Nirguna Mānasa Pūjā*, *Prapanchasāra Tantra*, *Ātmabodha*, *Manīshāpanchaka*, *Anubhava Pancharatna*, *Advaita*

*Bodhāmrita, Ātma-jnānopadesha-vidhi, Ātmānātma-
viveka, Ātmasāmrājya Siddhi, Harimīde Stuti* and
Mahāvākyārtha Vivarana.

Endowed with great evangelical zeal, he revived the
glory of the ancestral religion of the Hindus at a time
when the vast majority of Hindus had become followers
of the then-decadent Buddhism. He traveled throughout
the length and breadth of India preaching the message of
Advaita Vedānta and started four *maths* (monasteries) in
the four corners of India—one in Purī in the east, one in
Dwārakā in the west, one in Badarikā in the north, and
one in Rāmeswaram in the south. He is also the founder
of the famous Dashnāmī order of Hindu monks.

A man of gigantic intellect and blazing spirituality, he
also exemplified through his own life the ideals of *bhakti-
yoga, jnāna-yoga* and *karma-yoga* in the fullest measure.

At age 32 he passed away in the Himalayas at Kedār.
A small temple built on his grave attracts thousands of
pilgrims from all over India.

(8) Totakāchārya (7th century A.D.): He was one of the
foremost disciples of Shankarāchārya and is the author
of the book *Shrutisāra Samuddharana.*

(9) Padmapāda (7th century A.D.): He was among
the foremost disciples of Shankarāchārya. He wrote
a well-known commentary named *Panchapādikā* on
Shankarāchārya's commentary on the *Brahmasūtra*s.

(10) Mandana Mishra (7th century A.D.): His book *Brahmasiddhi* is considered one of the authentic books on *Advaita Vedānta*. He is also the author of *Sphotasiddhi*, *Vidhiviveka*, *Bhāvanāviveka*, and *Vibhramaviveka*. He was a disciple of Shankarāchārya.

(11) Sureshvara (A.D. 675-A.D. 773): One of the foremost disciples of Shankarāchārya, Sureshvara was the abbot of the Shringerī monastery for many years. He wrote a commentary on the *Brihadāranyaka Upanishad* containing 12,000 verses. Among his other books on *Advaita Vedānta*, *Naishkarmya-siddhi* is quite famous.

(12) Hastāmalaka (7th century A.D.): He was a disciple of Shankarāchārya and authored the *Hastāmalaka-stotra*. It is believed that his guru, Shankarāchārya, wrote a commentary on that book.

(13) Sarvajnātma Muni (8th century A.D.): A disciple of Deveshvara (Sureshvara?), he wrote an excellent book on *Advaita Vedānta* called *Samkshepa-shārīraka*. He authored two other books named *Pancha Prakriyā* and *Pramāna Lakshanam*.

(14) Vāchaspati Mishra (9th century A.D.): He was born in Mithilā. A great scholar, he wrote commentaries on different systems of Hindu philosophy. Among the books authored by him, his commentary on Shankarāchārya's commentary on the *Brahmasūtras* is very well known. He named the commentary after his wife, Bhāmatī. His other books are *Sānkhyatattva Kaumudī*, *Tattvavaishāradī*, *Tattvabindu*, *Nyāyakanikā* and *Brahmatattva Samīkshā*.

He also wrote a commentary called *Tātparya* on the *Nyāyavārtika* by Udyotkara.

He most probably had two gurus: Trilochana and Jayantabhatta.

(15) Yādavaprakāsha (11ᵗʰ century A.D.): He was a renowned professor of *Advaita Vedānta* in the city of Kānchī and wrote a commentary on the *Brahmasūtra*s. He was the guru of Rāmānujāchārya.

(16) Prakāshātma-yati (11ᵗʰ century A.D.): He wrote a famous commentary on the *Panchapādikā* authored by Padmapāda.

(17) Advaitānanda (12ᵗʰ century A.D.): Also known as Chidvilāsa and Ānandabodhāchārya, he was a disciple of Bhūmānanda, the abbot of the Kāmakoti monastery in Kānchī. He is the author of the books: *Brahmavidyābharana*, *Shānti Vivarana* and *Gurupradīpa*.

(18) Shrīharsha (12ᵗʰ century A.D.): He was a great logician and poet, besides being a scholar of *Advaita Vedānta*. His most famous book on *Advaita Vedānta* is *Khandana-khanda Khādya*.

(19) Ānandabodha Bhattāraka (12ᵗʰ century A.D.): A well-known scholar of *Advaita Vedānta*, he authored the books: *Nyāya-makaranda*, *Nyāyadīpāvalī*, *Pramānamāla* and a commentary on *Yogavāsishtha*.

(20) Ānandānubhavāchārya (12ᵗʰ century A.D.): He is the author of the book *Nyāyaratna Dīpāvalī*.

(21) Anubhūti Svarūpāchārya (13th century A.D.): He wrote the *Prakatārtha Vivarana*, a commentary on Shankarāchārya's commentary on the *Brahmasūtra*s. He also wrote commentaries on *Nyāyamakaranda* and *Nyāyadīpāvalī* by Ānandabodha Bhaṭṭāraka and Shankarāchārya's commentary on the *Māndūkya Upanishad*.

(22) Amalānanda Sarasvatī (13th century A.D.): He lived in Nāsikātryambaka on the bank of the river Godāvarī. He authored a book named *Vedāntakalpataru*, which is a commentary on the famous book *Bhāmatī* by Vāchaspati Mishra.

(23) Ānanda Pūrna Munīndra (13th century A.D.): Because of his scholarship he was given the title "Vidyāsāgara" (an ocean of knowledge). A disciple of Abhayānanda Sarasvatī, he wrote eight commentaries called *Vidyāsāgarī* on some famous books on *Vedānta*.

(24) Chitsukhāchārya (13th century A.D.): It is believed that he lived in Simhāchalam in Andhra Pradesh in South India. His book *Tattvapradīpikā* is quite well known. In scholastic circles it is known as *Chitsukhī*. Chitsukhāchārya was a prolific writer and wrote as many as fourteen books, most of which are commentaries on books authored by other renowned scholars of *Advaita Vedānta*.

(25) Jnānottama (13th century A.D.): He was the *guru* of Chitsukhāchārya and wrote the two books *Jnānasiddhi* and *Nyāyasudhā*.

(26) Rāmādvayāchārya (13th century A.D.): He is famous as the author of *Vedānta-kaumudī*.

(27) Vidyāranya Munīshvara (14th century A.D.): Celebrated in scholastic circles as the author of the books *Panchadashī, Sarvadarshana Sangraha, Jīvanmukti-viveka*, and *Vivarana-prameya-sangraha*, he wrote a total number of seventeen books.

(28) Shankarānanda (14th century A.D.): He was the *guru* of Vidyāranya. He wrote a commentary on the *Brahmasūtra*s called *Brahmasūtradīpikā*. He also wrote commentaries on the principal *Upanishad*s and the *Bhagavad Gītā*.

(29) Akhandānanda Sarasvatī (15th century A.D.): He wrote an elaborate commentary named *Tattvadīpana* on the *Panchapādikā Vivarana*.

(30) Ānandagiri (15th century A.D.): His *guru* was Shuddhānanda. He wrote several commentaries on different books. Among them, his commentaries on Shankarāchārya's commentaries on the *Bhagavad Gītā* and the Upanishads are quite famous.

(31) Prakāshānanda (15th century A.D.): His famous book is *Vedānta-siddhānta Muktāvalī*.

(32) Nrisimhāshrama (16th century A.D.): He was a renowned scholar of *Advaita Vedānta*. He authored the books *Advaitadīpikā, Tattvaviveka*, etc. His commentary on *Samkshepa Shārīraka* named *Tattvabodhinī* is quite fa-

mous. He also wrote a commentary on the *Padmapādikā Vivarana* named *Bhāva-prakāshikā*.

(33) Apyaya Dīkshita (16th century A.D.): He was a prolific author and wrote as many as 38 books. Among them *Siddhānta-lesha Sangraha* and a commentary named *Parimala* are well-known.

(34) Dharmarāja Advarīndra (16th century A.D.): His book *Vedānta Paribhāshā* is considered a very important piece of *Vedāntic* literature by scholars.

(35) Sadānanda Yogīndra (16th century A.D.): His book *Vedāntasāra* is very popular in *Vedānta* circles. Nrisimha Sarasvatī, Rāmatīrtha and Āpodeva have written commentaries on this book. Āpodeva's well-known commentary on *Vedāntasāra* is *Bālabodhinī*.

Among the other renowned teachers of *Advaita Vedānta* of the 16th century A.D. there were (36) Āpodeva, (37) Bhattojī Dīkshita, (38) Mallanārādhya, (39) Rangarāja Adhvarī, (40) Rāghavānanda Sarasvatī, (41) Balabhadra, (42) Venkatanātha, (43) Sadānanda Vyāsa and (44) Sadāshivendra Sarasvatī.

The best-known *Advaita* teachers of the 17th century A.D. are Madhusūdana Sarasvatī, Brahmānanda Sarasvatī, Kāshmīraka Sadānanda Yati, Govindānanda and Rāmatīrtha.

(45) Madhusūdana Sarasvatī was born in the village of Kotālipāra in the Faridpur county of East Bengal. His monumental work is *Advaitasiddhi*, written to refute the

objections about *Advaita Vedānta* contained in the book *Nyāyāmrita* by Vyāsatīrtha of the Madhvāchārya lineage. There is no subject in *Advaita Vedānta* that has not been discussed in the *Advaitasiddhi*. He also wrote the books *Siddhāntavindu*, *Advaitaratna-rakshana*, *Vedāntakalpalatikā*, *Gītāgūdārtha-dīpikā*, *Bhaktirasāyana* and a commentary on the *Samkshepa-shārīraka*.

(46) Brahmānanda Sarasvatī was a great scholar and wrote two excellent commentaries on Madhusūdana Sarasvatī's books, *Advaitasiddhi* and *Siddhāntavindu*.

(47) Kāshmīraka Sadānanda Yati is the author of a well-known book on *Advaita Vedānta* named *Advaita-brahma-siddhi*.

(48) Govindānanda wrote an excellent commentary titled *Ratnaprabhā* on Shankarāchārya's commentary on the *Brahmasūtra*s.

(49) Rāmatīrtha authored the famous commentary named *Vidvan-manoranjanī* on Sadānanda Yogīndra's *Vedāntasāra*.

(50) Achyuta Krishnānandatīrtha, (51) Nārāyana Tīrtha, (52) Rāmānanda Sarasvatī and (53) Lakshmīnrisimha are other well-known *Advaita* teachers of the 17th century A.D.

Among the *Advaita* teachers of the 18th century A.D. were (54) Āyannadīkshita and (55) Vith-thaleshopādhyāya.

In addition to the above, there are four teachers worth mentioning whose chronological details are not available. They are (56) Allāla Sūri, (57) Ādinārāyana, (58) Lakshmīdhara and (59) Sundarapāndya.

A more or less comprehensive list of the teachers of *Advaita Vedānta* is given above with the hope that the readers of this book may benefit from their teachings, if and when they develop further interest in a deeper study of *Advaita Vedānta*.

Srī Rāmakrishna (1836–1886)

APPENDIX 1

Some *Advaita* Thoughts as Expressed by Srī Rāmakrishna

"*Advaita* is the highest truth."

"*Brahman* alone is real, and the world illusory—I know this to be the essence of *Vedānta*."

"The individuals (*jīvas*) and the world (*jagat*) appear to exist but they don't have any real existence. As long as one has the "ego"—the sense of "I"—the individuals and the world seem to be there. When one kills the ego with the sword of Supreme Knowledge (the knowledge of *Brahman*), the individuals and the world cease to exist. One's ego is then proved to be as unreal as the magician's magic."

"The goal of *jnānayogīs* is to know their inherent divine nature. This is knowledge; this is liberation. Supreme *Brahman* (*Parabrahman*) is their True Nature. They and the Supreme *Brahman* (*Parabrahman*) are the same."

—Source: *The Gospel of Sri Ramakrishna.*

Swāmī Vivekānanda (1863–1902)

APPENDIX 2

Swāmī Vivekānanda's Thoughts on Unity Behind Diversity

"The theory of evolution, which is the foundation of almost all the Indian schools of thought, has now made its way into the physical science of Europe. It has been held by the religions of all other countries except India that the universe in its entirety is composed of parts distinctly separate from each other. God, nature, man—each stands by itself, isolated from one another; likewise, beasts, birds, insects, trees, the earth, stones, metals, etc., are all distinct from one another; God created them separate from the beginning.

"Knowledge is to find unity in the midst of diversity—to establish unity among things which appear to us to be different from one another. That particular relation by which man finds this sameness is called Law. This is what is known as Natural Law.

"I have said before that our education, intelligence, and thought are all spiritual, all find expression in religion. In the West, their manifestation is in the external—in the physical and social planes. Thinkers in ancient India gradually came to understand that that idea of separateness was erroneous, that there was a connection among all those distinct objects—there was a unity which pervaded the whole universe—trees, shrubs, animals, men, *Devas*, even God Himself; the *Advaitin* reaching the climax in this line of thought declared all to be but the manifestations of the One." "In reality, the metaphysical and the physical universe are one, and the name of this One is *Brahman*; and the perception of separateness is an error—they called it *māyā*, *avidyā* or nescience. This is the end of knowledge."

—Source: *Complete Works of Swami Vivekananda.*

RECOMMENDED READING

Books in English

Bhāskarānanda, Swāmī. *The Philosophical Verses of Yogavāsishtha*. English translation of *Yogavāsishtha-sāra* with commentary & Sanskrit text. Viveka Press, Seattle, 2007.

Chatterjee, Satishchandra & Datta, Dhirendramohan. *An Introduction to Indian Philosophy*. University of Calcutta.

Deussen, Paul. *Outlines of the Vedānta System of Philosophy according to Shankara*. Translated by J. H. Woods and C. B. Runkle, New York.

Grimes, John. *A Concise Dictionary of Indian Philosophy*. State University of New York Press, New York.

Hiriyanna, M. *Outlines of Indian Philosophy*. George Allen & Unwin Ltd., London.

Jagadānanda, Swāmī. *Upadesasahasri of Shankaracharya*. Sri Ramakrishna Math, Madras.

Mādhavānanda, Swāmī. *Brihadāranyaka Upanisad*. Sanskrit text and English translation of Shankarāchārya's commentary. Advaita Ashrama, Calcutta.

Mādhavānanda, Swāmī. *Vedantaparibhasa*. Sanskrit text and English translation. Advaita Ashrama, Calcutta.

Mādhavānanda, Swāmī. *Vivekachudamani*. Sanskrit text and English translation. Advaita Ashrama, Calcutta.

Mahādevan, T. M. P. *Gaudapada: A study in Early Advaita*. Madras University.

Muller, Max. *Three Lectures on Vedanta Philosophy*, London.

Nikhilānanda, Swāmī. *Atmabodha* (By Shankarāchārya). Sanskrit text and English translation. Sri Ramakrishna Math, Madras.

Nikhilānanda, Swāmī. *The Upanishads*. Four vols. Harper & Bros., New York

Nikhilānanda, Swāmī. *Vedantasara of Sadananda*. Sanskrit text and English translation. Advaita Ashrama, Mayavati, Almora, Himalayas.

Nikhilānanda, Swāmī. *The Gospel of Sri Ramakrishna*. English translation of *Sri Sri Ramakrishna Kathamrita*. Ramakrishna-Vivekananda Center, New York.

Nityaswarupānanda, Swāmī. *Ashtāvakra Samhitā*. Sanskrit text and English translation. Advaita Ashrama, Calcutta.

Vimuktānanda, Swāmī. *Aparokshanubhuti* (By Shankar-āchārya). Sanskrit text and English translation. Advaita Ashrama, Calcutta.

Vīreswarānanda, Swāmī. *Brahma-Sūtras*. Sanskrit text and English translation with notes. Advaita Ashrama, Calcutta.

Vivekānanda, Swāmī. *The Complete Works of Swami Vivekananda*. Advaita Ashrama, Calcutta.

Books in Bengali

Bhattāchārya, Shrīmohan & Bhattāchārya, Dinesh Chandra. *Bharatiya Darshana Kosha (Vedanta)*. Sanskrit College, Calcutta.

Chattopādhyāy, Amūlpada. *Advaitamritavarshini*. Sri Amulpada Smriti Sangha, Calcutta.

Dhīreshānanda, Swāmī. *Vedanta-Samjna-Malika*. Udbodhan Karyalay, Calcutta.

Ghosh, Tejomay. *Saral Vicharey Advaitavad*. Tejomay Ghosh, Calcutta.

Vishvarūpānanda, Swāmī. *Vedantadarshan* (with Shankara's commentary). Sanskrit text with Bengali translation and commentary by the author. Advaita Ashrama, Calcutta.

GLOSSARY

Abādhita: 1. Not contradicted. 2. Valid knowledge that has not been contradicted.

Ābhāsa-Vāda: The Theory of Appearance in *Advaita Vedānta*. According to this theory, the world and its individual beings are only appearances on *Brahman*.

Abhoktā: Non-enjoyer.

Abhyāsarūpā Samādhi: *Samādhi* needing repeated practice.

Adhikārī: 1. A competent/worthy student. 2. One who is competent to learn something.

Adhishthāna: The substratum. *Brahman* is the substratum underlying creation.

Āgama Pramāna: 1. Reliable testimony. 2. Also called *Shabda Pramāna*.

Advaita Vedānta: Non-dualistic school of *Vedānta* philosophy. It teaches the oneness of God, the soul and the universe. The chief exponents were Gaudapāda and Shankarāchārya.

Advaita: Non-dualism.

Agni: 1. Hindu god of fire. 2. Extremely subtle energy or intense heat. 3. The fire element.

Ajāta-vāda: The theory of Non-Origination that says that the perceptual world in which we exist was never created. This theory does not believe in causality.

Ajāti-vāda: Another name for the above. The theory of Non-Origination that says that the perceptual world in which we exist was never created. It has no source or cause.

Ajnāna: 1. Ignorance. 2. It also means the ignorance of the Ultimate Reality.

Ajnānī: One who is ignorant.

Ajnāta-Jnāpakam Shāstram: Literally, what makes the unknown known is a scripture.

Akāmahatah: Free from the desire for sense enjoyment.

Akartā: Non-doer.

Ākāsha: 1. One of the five subtle elements that have composed this world. 2. The "sky" element.

Ānandam: 1. Perpetual bliss. 2. One of the epithets of *Brahman*.

Anubandha: Indispensable requirement or essential qualification.

Anubhava: Personal experience.

Anumāna Pramāna: Inference as a source of valid knowledge.

Anupalabdhi Pramāna: Non-perception used as a method of determining valid knowledge.

Antah-karanam: Inner instrument of knowing. In plain language, the "mind."

Ap: 1. Literally, "water." 2. One of the five subtle elements that have composed this world.

Aparoksha Anubhūti: Direct experience.

Apparent self: The ego.

Ārambha-Vāda: 1. The theory that the effect is originally non-existent in the cause. According to this theory, the effect is something new produced by the cause. 2. Also called *Asatkārya-Vāda*.

Arthāpatti Pramāna: Postulation as a means of valid knowledge in the *Mīmāmsā* school and *Advaita Vedānta*.

Asamprajnāta Samādhi: Concentration par excellence. It is the highest spiritual state attainable through the practice of *yoga*.

Asatkārya-Vāda: The theory that the effect is non-existent in the cause. The effect is something new produced by the cause. Also called *Ārambha-Vāda*.

Asti: "Existence" aspect of *Brahman* as this world.

Atharva-Veda: One of the four *Veda*s.

Athena: Greek goddess of wisdom.

Ātman: 1. The individual soul. 2. Also called *Jīva* or *Jīvātman*.

Atīndriya Anubhūti: Supersensuous knowledge.

Ātman/Jīva: The individual soul.

Ātma-Jnāna: 1. Knowing one's indwelling Divine Self. 2.

Experiencing one's *Brahman*-ness.

Avachchheda-Vāda: The Theory of Limitation in *Advaita Vedānta*.

Avāntara-Mukti: Also called *Krama-Mukti*. Liberation in stages.

Āvarana-Shakti: The veiling power of *Māyā*.

Avidyā/Ajnāna: 1. Ignorance. 2. A term of *Vedānta* philosophy denoting ignorance, individual or cosmic.

Avidyā-Māyā: *Māyā* of ignorance.

Avrijinah: Free from sin.

Bhakti: Love of God.

Bhakti-Yoga: The path of devotion.

Bhāti: "Manifestation" aspect of *Brahman* as this world.

Bhāvarūpa: Of a positive character.

Bheda: A distinction.

Brahmā: *Saguna Brahman* or *Īshvara* has three basic aspects: (1) the creator aspect, (2) the preserver aspect and (3) the destroyer aspect. When *Īshvara* creates, He is called *Brahmā*.

Brahmacharya: Celibacy.

Brahma-Loka: The realm of *Saguna Brahman*.

Brahman: 1. The Absolute. 2. The Supreme Reality of Non-dualistic *Vedānta*.

Brahmanishtha: Centered in *Brahman*.

Brahma-sūtras: 1. Aphorisms on *Brahman*. 2. Also known as *Vedānta Sūtras*. They present the teachings of *Vedānta* in a systematic and logical order and were written by *Bādarāyana* (*Vyāsa*).

Brahmavid: A person who has experienced *Brahman*.

Brahmavid-vara: One superior to a *Brahmavid* is called a *Brahmavid-vara*. (See *Brahmavid*.)

Brahmavid-varīān: One who has attained a higher level of knowledge of *Brahman* than a *Brahmavid-vara*.

Brahmavid-varishtha: One whose mind has attained the highest level of knowledge of *Brahman*.

Bhāti: Manifestation aspect of *Brahman* as this world.

Buddhi: The determinative faculty of the mind, which makes decisions.

Chit: Consciousness.

Dahara-Vidyā: Ordinary people think that anything that is real must exist in time and space. They cannot comprehend *Nirguna Brahman*, which transcends time and space. To help such people, the *Chhāndogya Upanishad* instructs them to worship at first *Saguna Brahman* dwelling in the little space at the very core of the human heart. People, who meditate on *Saguna Brahman* in this manner, become able to experience the transcendental *Nirguna Brahman* gradually. The knowledge of this kind of worship and meditation of *Saguna Brahman* in the human heart is called *Dahara Vidyā*. As a result of this kind of worship, a worshipper, at the time of death, leaves the body through a certain artery in the head and going to *Brahma–Loka* (the realm of *Saguna Brahman*) ultimately attains the knowledge of *Nirguna Brahman* under the guidance of *Hiranyagarbha* (the highest created being through whom *Saguna Brahman* projects this world).

Darshana: 1. Seeing. 2. Directly experiencing. 2. Vision.

Drik-drishya-Viveka: The method of separating the knower from the objects known.

Drishti-Srishti-Vāda: The theory of "Perception is Creation" in *Advaita Vedānta*.

Efficient Cause: *Nimitta-Kāranam*.

Eka-Jīva-Vāda: Another name for *Drishti-Srishti-Vāda*.

Ekam-eva-advitīyam: One without a Second.

Guna: 1. Quality. 2. Any of the three constituent parts of *prakriti*.

*Guna*s: Plural form of "*guna*". See *Guna*.

Hiranyagarbha: The highest created being through whom *Saguna Brahman* projects this world.

Ishta-Loka: Abode of the Personal God such as that of *Vishnu*.

Īshvara: Same as *Saguna Brahman*. *Īshvara* is the creator, preserver, and destroyer of this world.

Jīva: 1. Literally, living being. 2. The individual soul, which in essence is no other than *Brahman*.

Jīvātman: 1. The individual soul.

Jīvanmukta: One who is liberated here and now.

Jīvanmukti: The state of a *jīvanmukta*. See *Jīvanmukta*.

Jnāna-virodhī: Literally, that which is opposite to knowledge.

Jnāna-Yoga: The path of philosophical inquiry that leads to the Ultimate Truth.

Kalpa: A periodic cycle of creation and dissolution.

Karma-Yoga: The path of right action that leads to God realization.

Krama-Mukti: Also called *Avāntara-Mukti*. Liberation in stages.

Lakshmī: The deity who gives wealth and prosperity.

Lesha Avidyā: Trace of ignorance.

Maheshvara: The destroyer aspect of *Īshvara* or *Saguna Brahman*.

Mananam: Contemplation on the truth/truths taught by the teacher.

Manas: The simple cognizing ability of the mind.

Māndūkya-kārikā: A commentary by Gaudapāda on the *Māndūkya Upanishad*.

Material Cause: *Upādāna-Kāranam*.

Māyā: 1. Lit. magic. 2. Same as *avidyā* or *ajnāna* in *Advaita Vedānta*.

Mīmāmsā: Name of a school of Hindu philosophy. Also known as *Pūrva-mīmāmsā*.

Mithyā: A lie.

Moksha/Mukti: Liberation after death.

Mumukshutvam: 1. The yearning to be free from all kinds of limitations. 2. The yearning for liberation from the cycle of repeated births and deaths.

Mūla-Avidyā: Primal Ignorance.

Mūlāvidyā: Primal Ignorance.

Nāma: "Name" aspect of *Brahman* as this world.

Nāsadīya-Sukta: A hymn in the *Rigveda*. This hymn is sometimes called the *Creation Hymn*.

Neo-*Vedānta* School: A sub-school of the *Vedānta* philosophy based on the teachings of Swāmī Vivekānanda.

Neptune: Roman god of the waters.

Nididhyāsanam: Deep contemplation.

Nimitta-Kāranam: The efficient cause.

Nirguna: 1. Devoid of qualities. 2. One which is beyond *sattva-guna, rajo-guna and tamo-guna*.

Nirguna Brahman: *Brahman* which is beyond the three *guna*s. (See *Nirguna*.)

Nirvikalpaka Pratyaksha: Indeterminate perception.

Nirvikalpa Samādhi: The highest state of mental concentration or *Samādhi* according to *Advaita Vedanta*.

Nyāya system: One of the six major systems of Hindu philosophy.

Original Ignorance: The ignorance about *Brahman* that seems to create this manifold universe.

Panchīkarana: The process of mixing the five subtle elements to produce the five gross elements.

Pāramārthika Sattā: Ultimate existence.

Paramātman: Supreme *Brahman*/*Nirguna Brahman*.

Parināma: The real transformation of the material cause into the effect such as milk becoming yoghurt.

Prakriti: Mother Nature *composed* of *rajo-guna, tamo-guna* and *sattva-guna*.

Pramā: Valid knowledge.

Pramāna: A source of valid knowledge.

Prātibhāsika Sattā: Apparent existence.

Pratibimba-Vāda: The Theory of Reflection in *Advaita Vedānta*.

Pratyaksha Pramāna: Perception as a source of valid knowledge.

Prayojanam: Necessity.

Prithivī: 1. Extremely fine solid matter. 2. Earth element.

Priya: The "dearness" aspect of *Brahman*.

Pūrva Mīmāmsā: A school of Hindu philosophy. Also known as *Mīmāmsa*.

Rahasya Vidyā: Secret science.

Rajo-guna: One of the three *guna*s of *prakriti*. It is characterized by activity, restlessness, the tendency to dominate over others. etc.; it also generates lustfulness, anger, etc.

Real Self: The Supreme Self or *Paramātman*.

Rigveda: 1. One of the four *Veda*s. 2. The most ancient scripture of Hinduism.

Rik-Veda: Same as *Rigveda*.

Ripe "I": Indwelling Divine Self.

Rita: The eternal moral order set into motion by *Īshvara*.

Rūpa: The "form" aspect of *Brahman* as this world.

Saguna: 1. Endowed with qualities. 2. Also that which has *sattva-guna, rajo-guna and tamo-guna*.

Saguna Brahman: *Brahman* associated with *sattva-guna, rajo-guna and tamo-guna*.

Sajātīya-bheda: The distinction between the same kind of objects.

Sālokya: Remaining in the abode or realm of personal God.

Sālokya-Mukti: The lowest level of liberation in the dualistic school of *Vedānta* (*Dvaita-Vāda*). The departed soul goes to the abode of the personal God and remains there blissfully enjoying His presence.

Sāma-Veda: One of the four *Veda*s.

Samādhānam: Concentration of the restrained mind on the study of the scriptures. Also means acquiring virtues such as modesty, humility and willingness to serve the teacher.

Sāmīpya: Closeness.

Sāmīpya-Mukti: The next to the lowest level of liberation in the dualistic school of *Vedānta* (*Dvaita-Vāda*). The departed soul enjoys the bliss of extreme proximity to the Personal God.

Samvandhva: Relationship of a scripture with its subject matter.

Sārūpya: Acquiring the form of someone else.

Sārūpya-Mukti: The second to the highest level of liberation in the dualistic school of *Vedānta* (*Dvaita-Vāda*). The departed soul acquires the form of the Personal God and enjoys intense bliss.

Sānkhya system: The most ancient among the six major systems of Hindu philosophy. Kapila is the founder of this school. This system does not believe in a creator God.

Sarasvatī: The goddess of learning.

Sat: 1. Eternity. 2. True existence.

Sat-Chit-Ānandam: Existence, Knowledge and Bliss aspects of *Brahman*.

Satkārya-Vāda: The theory in which prior to its manifestation, the effect exists in a latent state in the cause.

Sattā: Existence.

Sattva-guna: One of the three *guna*s that constitute *prakriti*.

Satyam: Truth.

Satyasya Satyam: Truth of all truths.

Savikalpaka Pratyaksha: Determinate perception.

Sāyujya-Mukti: The highest level of liberation in the dualistic school of *Vedānta* (*Dvaita-Vāda*). After death the departed soul becomes blissfully absorbed in the Personal God.

Shabda Pramāna: Reliable testimony.

Shama: The restraining of the outgoing mental tendencies.

Shārīraka-sūtra: Another name of the book *Brahmasūtra* authored by Vyāsa.

Shraddhā: 1. Implicit faith in the teacher. 2. Respect for the teacher verging on adoration or worship. 3. Self-confidence.

Shravanam: Lit. hearing. In the contest of *Vedānta* it means hearing the scriptures from the mouth of the teacher.

Shrotriya: One who is well versed in the Vedic knowledge.

Shruti: Reliable testimony of the *Veda*s.

Srishti-Drishti-Vāda: A theory that one can see or experience the world because it is *already* there. Its existence is not dependent on anyone's seeing or knowing it. Whether one experiences this world or not, it exists.

Sthitirūpā Samādhi: Stable *samādhi*.

Sukta: A hymn.

Supreme Self: *Nirguna Brahman*.

Sūtra: Aphorism.

Svagata-bheda: Distinction within oneself.

Tadākāra-kāritavat: Like something that has taken the form of something else.

Tadanukūla-Yukti: Reasoning conducive to the acquisition of true knowledge.

Tadviparīta-Yukti: Adverse reasoning meant to disprove religious truths.

Tamo-guna: One of the three constituent parts of *prakriti*. (Mother Nature)

Tat: 1. Sanskrit pronoun which means *that*. 2. Traditionally used to denote *Brahman* which is beyond gender.

Tulāvidyā: Relative or Secondary ignorance in *Advaita Vedānta*.

Tattva-darshana: Experiential knowledge of truth.

Titikshā: Forbearance.

Triputī: A triad such as the knower, knowledge and the object known.

Turīya: 1. The fourth experience. 2. Also means *Brahman*.

Unripe "I": Ego.

Upādāna-Kāranam: The material cause.

Upādhi: The limiting adjunct.

Upamāna Pramāna: Comparison as a means of acquiring valid knowledge.

*Upanishad*s: The highly philosophical part of the *Veda*s.

Upāsanā: Ritualistic worship, devotional practices and devotional meditation on the Personal God.

Uttara-Mīmāmsā: Another name for the *Advaita Vedānta* school of Hindu philosophy.

Vaisheshika System: One of the six major systems of Hindu philosophy. It accepts only inference and perception as sources of valid knowledge. Kanāda, the founder of this system, is accredited with the discovery of the particular (*vishesha*). According to him, all particulars are independent of one another and they are infinite in number. This school of philosophy is pluralistic and realistic.

Varuna: The Hindu god of waters.

Vāyu: 1. Hindu god of the winds. 2. A fine gaseous substance. 3. The air element.

Veda: Supersensuous eternal truths revealed to ancient Hindu sages.

Vedānta: One of the six major systems of Hindu philosophy.

Videha-Mukti: Total identification with *Brahman* acquired by a *jīvan-mukta* after death.

Vidyā-Māyā: Literally, illusion of knowledge. 2. Also that part of *māyā* that can liberate one from the grip of *māyā*.

Vikshepa-Shakti: The projecting power of *māyā*.

Vijātīya-bheda: Distinction between two different kinds of objects.

Vishnu: The preserver aspect of *Īshvara* or *Saguna Brahman*.

Vivarta: Apparent transformation.

Vivarta-Vāda: The theory of apparent transformation of *Brahman* into the world. The *Advaita Vedānta* School of philosophy holds this theory.

Vyāvahārika Sattā: Empirical existence.

Yoga System: One of the six major systems of Hindu philosophy.

Vyāsa: The word literally means "the divider." In the context of Hinduism it means the sage Vyāsa who collected and then divided the Vedic knowledge to create a four-volume book called the *Veda*s. Vyāsa's other name is Bādarāyana.

Vyuth-thāna: Coming down from *samādhi* to the level of awareness of this world.

Yajur-Veda: One of the four *Veda*s.

INDEX

A

INDEX

INDEX

P

INDEX

water
    element (*ap*), 109–110
    god of (Varuna), 98
    See also analogies
water buffalos, 20
witness, 81–82, 96

Y

Yājnavalkya, 85
Yajur-Veda, 43
yearning, 57–58, 69
yoga
    Advaita Vedānta school and *yoga,* 139
    bhakti-yoga, 139, 148
    jnāna-yoga, 139, 148
    karma-yoga, 139,148
    nirvikalpa samādhi called *asamprajnāta samādhi* by the *yoga*
        school, 35n
    one of six major systems of religious philosophy within
        Hinduism, 47
    Shankarāchārya and the *yogas*, 139, 148
    yoga school accepts three *pramānas*, 16n

About the Author

Swami Bhaskarananda was born and educated in India and joined the Ramakrishna Order as a monk in January 1958. He was attached to the Headquarters of the Order at Belur (near Calcutta) for 12 years before being posted to Seattle in 1974. He has been President of the Vedanta Society of Western Washington in Seattle since 1980. He is also the spiritual head of the Vedanta Society in Hawaii and the Vedanta Society in Vancouver (Canada). On invitation, the Swami has traveled extensively in the United States, Canada, Brazil, Argentina, Uruguay, England, France, Japan, Iceland, and the Netherlands, giving talks on Hinduism and other spiritual topics. He has also visited Myanmar, Thailand, China, Russia, New Zealand and Australia. He is a founding member and past President of the Interfaith Council of Washington State. He is the founder and editor-in-chief of the quarterly journal *Global Vedanta*.